Postcolonial Feminine Writing

Mine Sevinç

Postcolonial Feminine Writing

Bodies, Gazes and Voices

PETER LANG

**Bibliographic Information published by the
Deutsche Nationalbibliothek**
The Deutsche Nationalbibliothek lists this publication in the Deutsche
Nationalbibliografie; detailed bibliographic data is available online at
http://dnb.d-nb.de.

Library of Congress Cataloging-in-Publication Data
A CIP catalog record for this book has been applied for at the
Library of Congress.

ISBN 978-3-631-86123-3 (Print)
E-ISBN 978-3-631-85615-4 (E-PDF)
E-ISBN 978-3-631-86577-4 (EPUB)
10.3726/b18942

© Peter Lang GmbH
Internationaler Verlag der Wissenschaften
Berlin 2022
All rights reserved.

Peter Lang – Berlin · Bern · Bruxelles · Istanbul · New York · Oxford · Warszawa · Wien

This publication has been peer reviewed.

www.peterlang.com

Dedication

Dedicated to the Shahrazads among us for refusing to conform and making the world a better place

Preface

Postcolonial Feminine Writing explores how contemporary postcolonial women writers reclaim a new position of writing that I define as 'postcolonial feminine writing', which mirrors and transcends the storytelling of Shahrazad in terms of theme and structure. Postcolonial feminine writing as a concept is drawn out of Frantz Fanon's 'Algeria Unveiled', Hélène Cixous's 'The Laugh of Medusa' and Shahrazad's storytelling. The intersection of these theories and narrative styles allows for an interrogation into how it is not only possible for women writers to operate within patriarchal narrative discourse, but also how it is possible to undo and re-imagine the very norms of the patriarchal discourse from within. Thus, this concept offers an alternative to colonial and patriarchal discourses by questioning how non-Western women are denied access to voice as well as different power structures such as honour and the gaze and by seeking ways to move beyond these restrictions. I question the extent to which Shahrazad is employed as a liberating figure in contemporary postcolonial women's narratives.

The following chapters locate the potential of Shahrazadean narrative in Hanan al-Shaykh's *One Thousand and One Nights* (2011), Elif Shafak's *The Gaze* (2006), and *Honour* (2012) in order to challenge and re-imagine societal norms and structures. I argue that postcolonial feminine writing enables Shafak and al-Shaykh to re-create liberating spaces and rethink patriarchal literary discourses as embodied. By demonstrating how Shahrazad uses her body to access a narrative voice and intertwines narrative desire with sexual desire, I trace the potential of voice to the body through postcolonial feminine writing. Then, I identify how postcolonial feminine writing enables multiple and fluid gazing positions, allowing marginalised figures to be subjects of the gaze and re-define their gender and societal identities. By questioning the patriarchal binary oppositions of voice/silence and honour/shame, I explore how it is also possible for silence and shame to be alternative forms of communication. Consequently, I argue that postcolonial feminine writing enables temporary interventions into patriarchal and colonial discourses. It is the repetition of these interventions, albeit temporary, that undermines patriarchal power structures whilst re-inventing more subversive and liberating discourses as well as embodied potentialities.

Mine Sevinc
Guildford, 2020

Acknowledgments

My sincerest gratitude to everyone, who has been involved in the publication of this book.

First and foremost, 'a thousand and one' thanks go to Dr Donna McCormack, Dr Shazia Jagot and Prof Bran Nicol for their supervisory guidance throughout my PhD research, which forms the basis of this book. To Donna, I do not think I would have enough words to be able to thank you. You have always been my rock with your unending patience, support, and constructive criticism. Our discussions not only shaped my intellectual development, but also motivated me to aim for the better. And, my most heartfelt thanks to Dr Shazia Jagot and Prof Bran Nicol, who have been involved in my research at different times. I am very grateful for your incredible guidance. It has been an honour to work with you.

My sincerest thanks to Dr Claire Chambers and Prof Diane Watt, who provided thought-provoking and insightful feedback.

I was also very lucky to have great colleagues and friends, who have been there for me. Dr Emily Fisher, Dr Amy Morgan, thank you so much for our coffee breaks and giving me your friendship. And my dear Heather Ballantyne, you've been a godsend. Thank you for being my study buddy. I asked you so many questions, and you have always helped me without a single complaint and kept my morale high until the last moment. I would like to thank dear friends, who have not been immediately involved with the writing of this book, but were always reassuring and supportive. Dr Esra Kiraz (and sincerely sorry for infiltrating your dreams with my research), Dr Deniz Tosun, Dr Emre Demirci, Betül Türkmen, Olcay Dağdeviren Günay; Dr Rachel Marsh, Dr Danielle Dove, Helen Murray and Dr Eleanor March (with special thanks for Wednesday socials). I would like to extend my thanks to Dr Selçuk Sentürk, who inspired me to seek the publication of this book.

And many thanks to two of most influential educators in my life, my high school English tutor, Gülay Öztürk Turnagöl, without whose support I could not pursue English studies, and my undergraduate personal tutor, Dr Seval Arslan who helped me become the feminist I am today!

My dear (and not-so-much) patient parents, thank you for your support and encouragement and always welcoming me back home with much excitement and love! I love you both!

Last but not least, this monograph draws on research funded by Turkish Ministry of Education; I would like to express my gratitude for Turkish Embassy Education Counselling personnel.

Table of Contents

Introduction: Postcolonial Feminine Writing

All women speak two languages:
the language of men
and the language of silent suffering
Some women speak a third,
the language of queens
They are marvellous
and they are my friends

Mohja Kahf [1]

There is a tendency to assume all non-Western women are either silent sufferers or simply victims of their patriarchal cultures. Indeed, there is a third language that is neither simply 'the language of men' nor 'silent', but one which becomes 'the language of queens' precisely because it does not conform to any patriarchal literary conventions. This book explores contemporary postcolonial women's novels that resist the colonial, neo-colonial and patriarchal social norms which render non-Western women as silent and submissive figures. Rather, I aim to explore how contemporary postcolonial women writers reclaim a new position of writing, which mirrors and transcends the storytelling of Shahrazad, the most prominent Arabic female literary voice, in terms of themes, structure, narrative form and content.[2] I employ the image of Shahrazad the storyteller as the 'mistress' of literary discourse in this book to challenge and subvert the one-dimensionality of patriarchal narrative discourse.[3] I define this new form of narrative as postcolonial feminine writing and employ this concept as a theoretical framework and methodology for this book. As such, this book will demonstrate

---

1   Mohja Kahf, 'The Marvellous Women', "The Water of Hajar" and Other Poems: A Performance of Poetry and Prose, *The Muslim World*, 91, 1–2 (2001), pp. 31–44.

2   Shahrazad (or Scheherazade as commonly known by Western readers) is both a character and also the well-known narrator of *The Thousand and One Nights Tales*. I will refer to the tales as the *Nights* in future references. I choose the name 'Shahrazad' because 'Scheherazade' is a way of translators' domesticating the storyteller's name within the Western languages (i.e. German and English) and Shahrazad is the authentic Arabic usage.

3   I borrow the term 'mistress' for Shahrazad from Suzanne Gauch's *Liberating Shahrazad*.

how postcolonial feminine writing provides the potential for women writers to express agency through their novels arguing against the presumed silence of non-Western women. I will analyse Hanan al-Shaykh's *1001 Nights* (2011), and Elif Shafak's *The Gaze* (2006) and *Honour* (2012) in terms of how social and literary discourses such as narrative, the gaze, speech, silence and shame, which limit women's existences within pre-defined boundaries, are re-imagined insofar as women can 'get inside of' them and reclaim their own bodies and voices.[4]

This book argues that postcolonial feminine writing is a narrative form that contemporary postcolonial women writers employ to challenge and change patriarchal structures, that is, both societal norms and the very structures of narrative itself.[5] I suggest that postcolonial feminine writing as a concept is drawn out of Frantz Fanon's postcolonial theory in 'Algeria Unveiled' and Hélène Cixous's feminine writing theory, also known as *l'écriture feminine*, in 'The Laugh of Medusa'. More specifically, postcolonial feminine writing emerges at the intersections of feminine writing, Fanon's postcolonialism and the narrative of the *One Thousand and One Nights*. As I go on to demonstrate, Cixous and Fanon are important figures in considering postcolonialism and feminine writing separately but the intersection of these theories allows me to explore how it is not only possible for women writers to operate within patriarchal narrative discourse, but also how it is possible to undo and re-imagine the very norms

---

4   Hélène Cixous, 'The Laugh of Medusa', trans. by Keith Cohen and Paula Cohen, *Signs*, 1, 4 (1976), pp. 875–93, p. 887. I will refer to this essay as 'Medusa'.

5   Clearly, 'postcolonial feminine writing' is a broader concept than I aim to cover in this book. This concept extends across borders and contexts such as into Iraq and Palestine. There are a number of novels that can exemplify postcolonial feminine writing such as Ahmed Saadawi's *Frankenstein in Baghdad* (2018) and Sahar Khalifeh's *The End of Spring* (2004, 2008) in how they offer multiple perspectives, re-imagine social and gendered norms and present a repetitive and disruptive narrative. Although Saadawi's novel predominantly focuses on male characters, the main character is a queer monster named 'Whatsitsname'. While the narrative techniques used in *Frankenstein in Baghdad* such as repetitive and pluralistic narrative are postcolonial feminine, so is this monstrous figure, who shares with the public their own perspective; so, Whatsitsname figuratively occupies Shahrazad's position. Therefore, postcolonial feminine writing does not only navigate across borders, but it also engages with a present colonialism in the context of Palestine. Moreover, it is not merely a woman's concept of writing, but it is indeed feminine as it is not biologically deterministic in how it engages with gender and sex norms, as I discuss in relation to Cixous on pp. 35–6. However, my scope has been limited to three novels because I want to offer a nuanced and more in-depth analysis of the selected novels.

of the patriarchal discourse from within. Cixous attaches specific importance to writing and voice. As I explain later, she urges women to write, bring their bodies into the literary discourse, and have a voice. While this is a required and valid position, there are other mediums of expression for women that are not recognised by the patriarchal literary discourse.[6] When we look at the position of non-Western women and their writings, it is clear that they are denied access to writing and voice, not only because they are women, but because they are also of a non-Western race, nation and/or a different class. However, this does not mean they do not possess other forms of languages that allow them to challenge and undermine their restrictive social and literary boundaries. Here, the postcolonial context necessitates and helps us to look beyond the questions around women's writing and voice. Analysing feminine writing in a postcolonial context particularly requires recognising other mediums of communication such as silence and (un)veiling.[7] It becomes an alternative discourse to patriarchal and colonial discourses, similar to Shahrazad's storytelling, which builds on the acquisition of literary discourse with a claim to the area that is 'reserved [previously] for the great [men]'.[8] Building on this perception, postcolonial feminine writing allows us to interrogate how non-Western women are denied access to voice as well as different power structures such as honour and the gaze, and thus they seek alternative means of moving beyond the restrictions of these power structures. The logic of postcolonial feminine writing therefore is not confined to the medium of writing, but it is a multi-layered approach that recognises nuanced forms of expressions in contemporary postcolonial women's writing.

The concept of postcolonialism is not only a reference to the period after colonialism, as I will expand upon later, but it also connotes an ongoing (repetitive) practice, which both responds to neo-colonial and neo-imperial practices and refers to non-Western societies in terms of *representations, reading practices and values*.[9]

---

6   Here, I do not mean that the patriarchal literary discourse is simply a text written by male authors, nor do I suggest the notion of feminine writing merely belongs to female authors instead. I use 'the patriarchal literary discourse' to refer to the mainstream literature that centralises 'male privilege' and heteronormative gender mechanisms, which render women non-existent, as its focus in form and content. I will discuss 'male privilege' further in relation to Cixous on pp. 35–7 as it is central to understanding feminine writing.

7   I employ the term (un)veiling as a repetitive process of veiling and unveiling, and a form of disguise on p. 41-3.

8   Cixous, 'Medusa', p. 876.

9   John McLeod, *Beginning Postcolonialism* (Manchester: Manchester UP, 2000), p. 5.

Fanon's 'Algeria Unveiled' was written when Algeria was still a colony and fighting for national liberation. I choose Fanon's essay specifically because it is the first text to capture the intricate links between decolonisation and the undoing of gender and sexuality norms.[10] Therefore, it is a significant text that observes both the liberation process and predicts a liberated society, in which social and gender norms are subsequently expected to change. I will also demonstrate how 'Algeria Unveiled', which has been repeatedly condemned as sexist, also sought out to write in a language constrained by patriarchal norms, yet tried to imagine a society based on structures distinct from the colonial authority and male domination.[11] Fanon extensively describes how Algerian women fight in the war for national liberation and how their presence brings about changes in gender norms and values. As I go on to elaborate, Fanon argues that Algerian women 'reassumed and removed' their veils repeatedly during this process to seem to conform to colonial expectations, which in turn gave them the ability to transgress national and gender boundaries. This suggests that non-Western women used what inherently belonged to them: their bodies and bodily practices such as the veil and clothing to undermine colonial and gender norms. Moreover, I want to suggest how writing by a man similarly aims to undo the patriarchal ideals of colonial powers. Therefore, I would suggest that postcolonial feminine writing does not merely belong to women writers, but also to male writers, who challenge and rework patriarchal discourses.

Central to any rethinking of discourse as embodied, this book employs Cixous's essay when considering writing as emerging through embodiment, and as creating forms that challenge and reimagine patriarchal narrative forms. Cixous suggests women should write their bodies and bring their bodies back

---

10 Lindsey Moore argues that Fanon's text is 'distinguished by its attention to women's flexible resistance to the colonial gaze and power/ knowledge apparatus' and therefore it offers 'a template' to read women as *signifying agents*. Lindsey Moore, '"Darkly as through a Veil": Reading Representations of Algerian Women', *Intercultural Education*, 18, 4 (2007), pp. 335–51, pp. 340–1. Also, Robert J.C. Young asserts that the theorisation of postcolonialism has started with Frantz Fanon. See Robert J. C. Young, 'What is the Postcolonial', *ARIEL*, 40, 1 (2009), pp. 13–25, p. 16.

11 My reading of Fanon does not disregard the fact that women do not have defined voices in 'Algeria Unveiled'. However, I want to acknowledge that this text dramatically differs from his earlier works such as *Black Skins* insofar as the essay centralises women's militancy into national liberation as well as changing gender dynamics. While I recognise it may not be Fanon's intention, not incorporating women's voices demonstrates the difficulty of defining 'a feminine practice of writing' within pre-defined patriarchal terms and thus it contributes to my conception of postcolonial feminine writing.

to narrative because the patriarchal narrative discourse neglects the existence of otherness and femininity. According to Cixous, the inclusion of women's bodies within patriarchal literary discourse deconstructs this discourse and provides 'immense resources' to be discovered.[12] Cixous brings women and bisexuality to the fore of her narratives, and I engage with her work precisely because the literary texts which I analyse tackle such issues as gender norms and women's voices through creative and alternative narrative forms and subject matters. I incorporate Cixous and Fanon into postcolonial feminine writing because these theories complement each other and allow me to investigate how (un) veiling is fundamentally a woman's bodily practice and a way for women to exist both physically and mentally in patriarchal and postcolonial discourses. (Un) veiling first occurs on and through the body and it presents Algerian women with the potential for changes to gender values within the society. By bringing their bodies into the context of war, Algerian women become important agents for the national cause and signify great possibilities for the future of the liberated nation in terms of repeatedly (un)veiling gender norms. Whilst the literary texts and national contexts that I engage with bear little relation to Algeria, I consider Fanon's engagement with decolonisation and gender norms as central to the textual practice of both al-Shaykh and Shafak. Here, I do not want to suggest that all postcolonial contexts are the same by centralising Fanon's discussion of Algerian decolonisation, but to show how the varying contexts can engage with similar issues in different manners. Indeed, I want to point out that colonisation can happen on many levels such as neo-imperialism and immigration policies. Both Turkey and Lebanon have gone through a process of colonialism and national liberation during different time periods. While this form of colonialism has similarities for both countries in terms of the colonisers (initially by the Ottoman Empire and later England and/or France), the process of decolonisation was highly different especially considering Turkey gained independence decades earlier. Also, the change of political regime after decolonisation is telling. While Turkey became a secular republic and overlooked religious and ethnic differences, Lebanon became a religion-based republic.[13] Furthermore, the Algerian context is not the first one to engage with women's liberation incorporated into national liberation.

---

12 Cixous, 'Medusa', p. 880.
13 This multiplicity of religious sects and the Israeli-Palestinian conflict (Palestinian refugees in Lebanon) gave rise to political unrest, which came to be known as Lebanese Civil War between the years 1975 and 1990. In the aftermath of the war, Lebanon went under the mandate of Syria until 2005.

For instance, many Turkish critics such as Yesim Arat and Deniz Kandiyoti argue for the heterogeneity of the veil and highlight how it has held a significant space in Turkish revolutions (1919–1934).[14] Kandiyoti specifically explains how the Turkish revolution made women battlegrounds for social and national reforms by defining a new Turkish woman and grounding this image as the basis of a new liberated Turkish society.[15]

Turning to Shahrazad, I develop the link between these major philosophers because she is the central figure in my selected novels which exist in the post-colonial contexts I have discussed. Therefore, my concept emerges from these literary texts, to argue that literature helps us to develop theoretical thinking on how societal constraints may be undermined and re-formed. Shahrazad is first and foremost a character and the king's new bride in the *Nights*. She asks for the king's permission to begin a story the first night and continue telling her stories for an infinite period of time. Here, I refer to the position of Shahrazad in contemporary postcolonial narratives and point out the difference from previous narratives in many ways. With no particular origin, the *Nights* involving Shahrazad were not complete versions and they were largely ignored by the Arab literati because they were part of an oral tradition.[16] The Western translations of *The Arabian Nights* aimed to reflect an idea of the East and produce 'a full, complete, unvarnished, uncastrated copy of the great original'.[17] The translators adapted the stories to include an epilogue in which Shahrazad is pardoned by the king and becomes his wife. This created an ordered text and effectively limited Shahrazad's storytelling within patriarchal literary boundaries. Therefore, contemporary postcolonial writers return to this text and adapt and recreate Shahrazad in their works to free her from these colonial and patriarchal boundaries. As I will explore later, Shahrazad's mission is double in challenging both domestic and Western/colonial restrictions. I also point out the endless potential that Shahrazad's storytelling presents by referring to the tales as the *1001 Nights*, which connotes repetition and potential for change, instead of the Orientalist

---

14 The process of Turkish revolutions covers a long period of time as well as a range of areas from political changes such as the capitalisation of Ankara to gender and conjugal norms such as the abolition of polygamy.

15 Deniz Kandiyoti, 'End of Empire: Islam, Nationalism and Women in Turkey', in *Women, Islam and the State*, ed. by Deniz Kandiyoti (Philadelphia, PA: Temple UP, 1991), pp. 22–47.

16 Husain Haddawy, 'Introduction', in *The Arabian Nights*, ed. by Muhsin Mahdi (New York and London: W. W. Norton & Company, 1990), p. xviii.

17 Ibid., p. xxvii.

and confining title the *Arabian Nights*.[18] Thus, the intersection between Shahrazad, Cixous and Fanon offers a route to explore how women's bodily and mental existences in the patriarchal literary discourse open up the potential for change to gender norms and literary discourses. Therefore, postcolonial feminine writing allows me to investigate how different social norms and values restricting women such as the gaze, silence and honour can also be re-imagined in al-Shaykh's and Shafak's novels as forms of Shahrazad's re-narratives.

Before moving on to discuss postcolonial feminine writing further, it is useful to identify what I mean by 'Shahrazad's re-narratives'. I read along similar lines to Suzanne Gauch in that we both interpret a variety of texts in terms of a revival of Shahrazad in several ways.[19] I analyse novels, which are a re-writing of her tales with a specific focus on gender violence (al-Shaykh's re-imagining of the *Nights*), a re-writing of Shahrazad's figure as the storyteller (Esma in *Honour*), and a re-writing of the dynamics of power systems (the various forms of gazing positions in *The Gaze*). These novels specifically replicate Shahrazad's own disruptive capabilities. Therefore, I have chosen my texts specifically with a focus on how they incorporate Shahrazad's storytelling. I am also interested in broadening the ways in which Shahrazad is considered as a non-Western figure and consequently analyse Lebanese and Turkish authors together to point out that Shahrazad's cultural heritage belongs to no specific nation or race. In doing so, postcolonial feminine writing navigates across national borders. While the *Nights* is formerly a collection of tales from throughout the Middle East, the recognition of Shahrazad as a liberating figure is common in both Lebanese and Turkish writers' texts. As both Lebanon and Turkey descend from the late Ottoman Empire, the trope of Shahrazad stands a transnational inheritance, native to Turkish, Persian Lebanese and several other Arabic countries. Thus, the tradition of Shahrazad's storytelling is reproduced in both Shafak and al-Shaykh's texts to challenge both national/domestic and Western/colonial restrictions.

---

18 The title *Arabian Nights* disregards the range of geographical origins that contribute to a variety of tales, and fails to recognise the repetitiveness of the tales, which is one of the most significant aspects of the *Nights* in prolonging the process of storytelling and postponing the storyteller's death. This title also infers an Orientalist fantasy of appropriating the East as 'feminine' through the image of Shahrazad. Therefore, the *Arabian Nights* becomes another way of undermining the complexity of image of the East and the *Nights*.

19 Suzanne Gauch, *Liberating Shahrazad: Feminism, Postcolonialism and Islam* (Minneapolis, MN: The University of Minnesota Press, 2007), p. xiv.

The purpose of this book is to look at the figure of Shahrazad in a transnational context in *1001 Nights* by al-Shaykh, and *The Gaze* and *Honour* by Shafak. I have chosen these novels precisely because they incorporate Shahrazad's storytelling as a form of re-narrative. While Shafak and al-Shaykh both construct a tension between gender and nationhood in their narratives, they also demonstrate 'multiple attachments' to norms of nation, ethnicity and race.[20] That is, they both currently reside in London and refuse to be symbols of their nations. Therefore, both writers dwell the position of diasporic women writers, and are often racialised and discriminated. Due to the liminality of their diasporic experiences, Shafak and al-Shaykh are, nevertheless, in a unique position to offer nuanced analyses of both national and universal literary contexts. Both writers raise similar issues of racialised and gendered experiences when they are interviewed: Al-Shaykh verbalises her concerns: 'it bothers me that [the western media] want[s] me to be a spokesperson for Arab women and I have refused in various circumstances'.[21] Along similar lines, Shafak utters her concern in her TEDTalk: 'If you're a woman writer from the Muslim world, like me, then you are expected to write the stories of Muslim women and, preferably, the unhappy stories of unhappy Muslim women. You're expected to write informative, poignant and characteristic stories and leave the experimental and avant-garde to your Western colleagues'.[22] Accordingly, Shafak's various novels offer insight into both local Turkish characters as well as multiple international and migrant others in transnational and transhistorical contexts. Even though al-Shaykh primarily focused on the Lebanese Civil War in her earlier novels, as a Lebanese author who is concerned with her war-torn nation, she also reflects on various themes in her later works.[23] Therefore, both writers challenge and respond to Western traditions of storytelling, which tend to undermine diasporic women's writing. While their novels emerge from different national contexts, they can be contextualised as both local and universal. For this reason, I do not want to focus specifically on their texts in their respective national contexts, but I want

---

20 Elif Shafak, 'The Revolutionary Power of Diverse Thought', *TEDTalk*, September 2017, <https://www.ted.com/talks/elif_shafak_the_revolutionary_power_of_diverse_thought?language=en> [accessed 10th January 2020].

21 Anna Ball, 'Things That Walk with Me: Hanan Al-Shaykh in Conversation', *Wasafiri*, 26, 1 (2011), pp. 62–66, p. 63.

22 Elif Shafak, 'The Politics of Fiction', *TEDTalk*, July 2010, <https://www.ted.com/talks/elif_shafak_the_politics_of_fiction> [accessed 28th December 2019].

23 For instance, both *Only in London* (2001) and *The Occasional Virgin* (2018) contextualise migration and transgression of several gender, sexual and social class norms.

to investigate how they address broader topics in their novels through the figure of Shahrazad. I would suggest that both writers use Shahrazad's re-narrative to consider patriarchal systems of power as restrictive to both men and women.[24]

While these novels have similarities in terms of structure and literary focus, they also expand and carry Shahrazad's legacy forward in the ways they re-imagine liberating spaces and engage with various social and gender norms. Most recently, Shafak wrote an article introducing the concept of a liberating space for her writing.[25] She explains that 'the Mount Qaf' is 'a land of undisturbed peace, justice, equality, [and] freedom. An elsewhere. It was called "that which lies behind Mount Qaf"'.[26] Shafak explains that what draws her to the existence of this 'elsewhere' is that it is 'a place of endless possibilities and uncensored words – a source of diversity, creativity, [and] imagination. It held the keys to Storyland. It provided a sense of empowerment to the powerless'. While 'the Mount Qaf' provides the possibility of endlessness and limitless imagination, it is also 'invisible on any map'. Therefore, it is not simply possible for everyone to access this space and it does not mean that the land of endless possibilities does not exist just because everyone cannot find it. The notion of 'the Mount Qaf' indicates the existence of a liberating space that allows for undoing socio-cultural norms. 'The Mount Qaf' is also a significant setting for the *Nights*, which allows for re-imagining social and gender boundaries. I would therefore point out that the incorporation of Shahrazad's storytelling within postcolonial feminine writing allows Shafak and al-Shaykh a space of uncensored possibilities in 'Storyland'. This notion of 'elsewhere' opens up the potential for re-learning and re-imagining various power dynamics in a postcolonial context.[27]

---

24 Al-Shaykh is concerned with how '[women] are victims of society more than victims of men because men are sometimes victims of society as well' [Paula Sunderman, 'An Interview with Hanan al-Shaykh', *Michigan Quarterly Review*, 31, 4 (1992), pp. 625–36, p. 629]. Along similar lines, Shafak offers a complicated observation of social and gender norms by cross-dressing as the male protagonist (Alex) on the cover of *Honour* and reflects on the victimisation of Alex via patriarchal norms of family honour.

25 Elif Shafak, 'As a Lost Child in Turkey I Found Refuge on an Imaginary Mountain', *The Guardian*, 26th August 2019, <https://www.theguardian.com/commentisfree/2019/aug/26/lost-child-turkey-refuge-imaginary-mountain>[accessed 5th December 2019].

26 Ibid.

27 I explore postcolonialism as re-learning in relation to Robert J. C. Young's article on p 23.

Re-writing the Postcolonial

Postcolonialism has been a controversial term because of the lack of clarity as to what it refers. Bill Ashcroft, Gareth Griffiths and Helen Tiffin suggest that the postcolonial should be analysed in an historical linearity that includes pre-colonial, colonial and post-colonial periods and that 'the post-colonial is still best employed […] to refer to post-*colonization*'.[28] Although Ashcroft et al acknowledge the problem of linearity that postcolonialism initially 'sets out to dismantle',[29] they still endorse the linearity by hyphenating the term 'post-colonial' – to focus on the colonial period as an historical fact – and prioritising the post-colonial that 'first emerged […] in the cultural discourse of formerly colonized peoples'.[30] I agree with Ashcroft et al that postcolonial theory is embedded in and indebted to colonial discourse in one respect. However, I would argue that the over-emphasis on colonialism within the postcolonial context simply reproduces Euro-centricity, and thus primarily fetishizes colonial history over local and national agendas. Moreover, a chronological postcolonial analysis suggests a set period of colonialism and therefore overlooks the possibility of neo-colonial and neo-imperial experiences.[31] Likewise, Sara Ahmed focuses on the impossibility of the term 'post-coloniality', which assumes the legacy of colonialism is simply overcome. Ahmed suggests that postcolonialism is 'about the complexity of the relationship between the past and present, between the histories of European colonisation and contemporary forms of globalisation'.[32] The postcolonial is this 'complexity' that problematizes the understanding of both past and present in terms of colonisation and globalisation. While the postcolonial suggests that the

---

28 Bill Ashcroft et al, *The Empire Writes Back: Theory and Practice in Postcolonial Literatures* (London and New York: Routledge, 1989, 2002, 2004), p. 195, emphasis in original.

29 Anne McClintock, *Imperial Leather: Race, Gender and Sexuality in the Colonial Contest* (New York: Routledge, 1995), p. 10, also quoted in Ashcroft et al., *The Empire Writes Back*, p. 195.

30 Ibid., p. 196.

31 This can better be understood in the context of contemporary international politics and Donald Trump's travel ban on Arab countries restricting their entry to the US on a security pretext. Similarly, the contemporary British PM Boris Johnson criticises Muslim women for wearing hijabs and 'looking like letter boxes'. 'Boris Johnson's burqa jibe' BBC, 8 August 2018 https://www.bbc.co.uk/news/uk-45112792 [last accessed 15 August 2019].

32 Sara Ahmed, *Strange Encounters: Embodies Others in Post-coloniality* (London: Routledge, 2000), p. 11.

colonial past and the present are intertwined, it also indicates that the present is not 'simply continuous with the past'.[33] Ahmed therefore argues that 'post-coloniality' becomes the space that allows us to interrogate the significance of 'colonial encounters' in history as well as the inability of these colonial histories in determining local and social contexts.

Building on Ahmed's notion of 'post-coloniality', I want to re-formulate understandings of the postcolonial within my theoretical and literary analyses. The term postcolonial has been used in very particular ways to refer to the colonial past.[34] However, the end of active colonisation does not mean the end of orientalism or neo-imperialism. Postcolonialism therefore cannot be understood as a completed process nor as an end to the colonial period. Rather, it is a continuing practise in the face of these attacks to which postcolonial women writers respond with their novels. Robert J. C. Young suggests that it is very possible 'not [to] identify yourself as western, or as somehow not completely western even though you may live in a western country'.[35] Then, postcolonialism offers the opportunity to '[see] things differently, a language and a politics in which your interests come first, not last'.[36] Young argues that postcolonial allows those who occupy positions of power to 'relearn and return to the ordinary world for re-education'.[37] Thus, it becomes possible to identify as *somehow* Western and still to be able to critique from a postcolonial perspective. Although literature may be considered as central to understanding this notion of postcolonialism, it further opens up the 'analyses of objective historical processes with the subjective experience of those who undergo them' for question.[38] Therefore, I would argue that postcolonialism becomes a reading and re-learning practice that is not simply for literature. Postcolonialism proposes the occasion to re-read histories and bodies by de-centring the Western perspective from the critical investigation of the relationship between the coloniser and the colonised, as well as

---

33 Ibid., p. 11.
34 In addition to Bill Ashcroft, Hellen Tiffin and Gareth Griffiths's *The Empire Writes Back* (2004), Stuart Hall's 'When was "the Post-Colonial": Thinking at the Limit' (1996), Ania Loomba's *Colonialism/Postcolonialism* (2005) and Elleke Boehmer's *Colonial and Postcolonial Literature* (2005) concentrate predominantly on the importance of the colonial past in postcolonial criticism.
35 Robert J. C. Young, 'What is the Postcolonial', *ARIEL*, 40, 1 (2009), pp. 13–25, p. 16.
36 Ibid., p. 16.
37 Ibid., p. 17.
38 Ibid., p. 16.

issues ranging from race, immigration, hybridity, belonging, resistance, multi-culturalism to intersectionality.[39]

Colonisation may happen on many levels. The liminal position of Turkey would be an example of how postcoloniality goes beyond the experience of political colonisation. Although Turkey has not been politically colonised, and indeed descends from an imperial power, the Ottoman Empire, its fluctuating political and social position with respect to the West necessitates a postcolonial analysis. Mainly because Turkey's position has always been geographically and politically unstable, it holds a liminal space as the bridge between the West and the non-West. After the multi-ethnic Ottoman Empire was dissolved during the War of Independence (1919–1922), Turkey was founded as a nation-state with strictly nationalist ideals. Hamit Bozaslan argues that 'the War of Independence was not only a struggle against the European powers which tended to destroy Turkey and "Turkishness", but also a war of emancipation from the Ottoman yoke. By extension, it was considered as the very prototype of anti-imperialist and anti-colonial wars'.[40] To reflect late Ottoman Empire as colonial and the War of Independence as against colonial powers, Turkey can be still considered in a postcolonial context despite not being claimed as a European colony. While this War of Independence rejected Western colonisation on post-Ottoman lands, the Republic of Turkey appropriated Western law, education and lifestyle as an ideal. Elena Furlanetto argues that Turkey went through a 'perceived colonization' as part of the 'massive Westernization process enacted by Kemalism [which is an ideological pursuit of Kemal Ataturk, the founder of the Republic of Turkey] in the attempt to inscribe Turkey into a Western narrative of progress and secularism'.[41] Therefore, Westernisation was imposed by Ataturk as the principal project of modernisation against the Ottoman practices. The proclamation of the Republic of Turkey does not necessarily put an end

---

39 For example, Aijaz Ahmad makes relevant links between colonialism and capitalism, modernity, Westernisation and social class in 'The Politics of Literary Postcoloniality'. Aijaz Ahmad, 'The Politics of Literary Postcoloniality', Race & Class, 36, 3 (1995), pp. 1–20.

40 Hamit Bozaslan, 'Turkey: Postcolonial discourse in a non-colonised state', in A Historical Companion to Postcolonial Literatures: Continental Europe and Its Empires, ed. by Prem Poddar et al. (Edinburgh: Edinburgh UP, 2008), pp. 423–4.

41 Elena Furlanetto, '"Safe Spaces of the Like-Minded": the Search for a Hybrid Post-Ottoman Identity in Elif Shafak's The Bastard of Istanbul', Commonwealth Essays and Studies, 36, 2 (2014), pp. 19–31, p. 20.

to ideological colonization even if it brings national sovereignty. This 'perceived colonization' leads to the repeated reproduction of power hierarchies between Turkey and the West as gendered and multiple. Although the War of Independence reflected Western colonisation as hostile and imperial, Turkey as a nation-state re-defined the West as a teacher and an ideal to be followed. Ali Bilgiç discusses how 'the West can be reproduced within non-Western states as an ideal to be reached, an example to follow, and sometimes a threat to be feared' and that this process is gendered in a way that masculinises the West while feminises the non-West.[42] It would therefore need a postcolonial feminist analysis to interrogate Turkey's forever liminal position as the weaker non-Western and feminine Other. It is no wonder that Elif Shafak responds to this 'perceived colonization' in her texts by challenging the binary of the East and the West and re-imagining embodied pasts, presents and futures. Shafak, I would suggest, attempts to re-capture a 'post-Ottoman identity', whereby it is possible to re-imagine the multi-ethnic, heterogenous Ottoman past in contemporary nation-state Turkey. For instance, Shafak's *The Bastard of Istanbul* (2006) contextualises post-Ottoman Armenian identities and their trauma of the past, which is reproduced by the younger generation's visit to contemporary Turkey. Similarly, *Honour* (2012) largely focuses on a multi-ethnic Turkish-Kurdish family and re-conceptualises more multicultural identities in the wake of Turkish Westernisation. In doing so, Shafak demonstrates how the present is still very much 'haunted' by the intricate colonial history of Turkey.

Lebanon's postcoloniality is just as complex and problematic. Initially colonised by the Ottomans, Lebanon is recognised as a state only after World War I as a result of the decline and unavoidable dissolution of the Ottoman Empire. As WWI led to the riots of Arab societies in the Ottoman lands supported by Britain, Britain and France gained more control of the Middle East and North Africa. The Arab riots were not repaid by 'the Arab homeland promised'.[43] Rather, the control of the area was dictated by Sykes-Picot agreement (1916) and Balfour Declaration (1917), which also gave birth to a Jewish settlement in Palestine and thus resulted in a formation of Palestinian refugee camps in Lebanon. With the formal recognition of mandates, the

---

42 Ali Bilgiç, *Turkey, Power and the West: Gendered International Relations and Foreign Policy* (I.B. Tauris: London and New York, 2016), Kindle, location 469.

43 Lindsey Moore, *Arab, Muslim, Woman: Voice and Vision in Postcolonial Literature and Film* (Abingdon and New York: Routledge, 2008), p. 26.

Christian-populated area is disunited from Syria as Lebanon and both undergo French mandates. Even though Lebanon can be recognised as postcolonial due to the French mandate of Syrian and Lebanese lands, the colonial history is less visible in contemporary Lebanon than the impact of the Lebanese Civil War (1975–1990). Bernard Lewis describes the 'horrors of Lebanese civil war [as] a situation where [...] even the law of the jungle was not respected'.[44] Lewis considers it difficult for Western reporters to understand the complexities of the civil war because 'such Western terminology cannot describe, still less explain, a conflict in which, in most domestic situations, the rival factions would define themselves as Catholic or Orthodox rather than Christian, Sunni or Shia rather than Muslim, and any of these rather than Lebanese'.[45] While this complexity is difficult to capture in Western terminology, it requires a postcolonial perspective to be able to capture these intricacies of cultural pluralisms within the bitter history of colonialism and civil wars. Sune Haugbolle argues that Lebanese Civil War holds a more prominent position in both Lebanese history and literature due to the lack of a strong Lebanese state.[46] As such Lebanese Civil War still stands as the very object of trauma and haunts both the public and private memories because '[i]t displays the tension between the need for remembering and that for forgetting the atrocities'.[47] Syrine Hout suggests that one of the most significant results in the post-war period is the rise of diasporic Anglophone Lebanese narratives.[48] Elise Salem argues that diasporic authors 'broadened and complicated the notion of Lebanon' by going beyond Lebanon's geographical and more importantly literary borders.[49] In the wake of developing Anglophone Lebanese writing, it is highly significant to recognise the position of diasporic women writers, such as Hanan al-Shaykh, who still prefers writing in Arabic. Al-Shaykh holds a unique position in Lebanese literature by dwelling in a diasporic position and reflecting on the cultural complexity and diaspora experience in her contemporary writings mostly in Arabic and except for the re-writing of *1001 Nights*. In doing so,

---

44 Bernard Lewis, *The Multiple Identities of the Middle East* (New York: Schocken Books, 1998, 1999), p. 104.

45 Ibid., p. 17.

46 Sune Haugbolle, *War and Memory in Lebanon* (Cambridge: Cambridge UP, 2010), p. 6.

47 Syrine Hout, *Post-war Anglophone Lebanese Fiction: Home Matters in the Diaspora* (Edinburgh: Edinburgh UP, 2012).

48 Ibid., p. 3.

49 Elise Salem, 'Patricia Sarrafian Ward, *The Bullet Collection*', *Literary Review*, 46, 4 (2003), pp. 769–70, p. 770.

al-Shaykh perpetually reproduces complex characters, who can transcend the very national, gender and social norms that are presumed restrictive in the post-war period.

Since 'the colonial past' is still present and haunting the present of both Turkish and Lebanese societies, it creates a repeated image of history that reiterates Orientalism and requires to be analysed with a more specific definition of postcolonialism. Michael O'Riley argues that Orientalism continues to be 'a fixed point of reference in postcolonial criticism, reappearing in the form of past images and fantasies to haunt the contemporary cultural scene'.[50] This understanding of orientalism leads to a tension between the understanding of postcolonialism as a linear process and continuing projects of orientalism. The image of haunting in postcoloniality is significant specifically because 'the invisible yet perceived persistence of a colonial past and desire linked to orientalist practice continues to condition both postcolonial [practices and] critical responses to them'.[51] Building upon O'Riley's discussion of a haunted postcolonialism, Anastasia Valassopoulos discusses the way postcolonial studies engages with both the understanding of the colonial past and the construction of a 'postcolonial consciousness' by seeking to expose how '(repressed histories of colonialism) are always retrievable, reparable and comprehensible'.[52] Therefore, it is significant that contemporary postcolonial writers return to the *Nights* because they are initially a product of a form of imperialism that still persists. The Western translations shape Shahrazad's storytelling and claim authority over the collection, order and conception of the *Nights*. This authority and these limitations are challenged by contemporary postcolonial women writers in refocusing on Shahrazad's image in their texts. I would therefore suggest that this contemporary return to Shahrazad, the most prominent Arabic storyteller from tenth century, is ultimately a response to the way histories and texts are haunted and maintained. Indeed, it is a political as well as a literary decision to incorporate Shahrazadean storytelling in postcolonial feminine writing because texts and languages are also haunted by this restrictive past and need to be re-visited by reviving Shahrazadean textual practices.

---

50 Michael O'Riley, 'Specters of Orientalism in France, Algeria, and Postcolonial Studies', *Mosaic*, 34, 4 (2001), pp. 47–64. p. 48.

51 Ibid., p. 48.

52 Anastasia Valassopoulos, *Contemporary Arab Women Writers: Cultural Expression in Context* (London and New York: Routledge, 2007), p. 134.

The One Thousand and Second Night of Shahrazad's Storytelling[53]

Postcolonial Feminine Writing suggests contemporary postcolonial women writers 'can make [the language theirs], containing it, taking it in [their] own mouth, biting that tongue with [their] very own teeth to invent for [themselves] a language to get inside of'.[54] In doing so, they 'make it possible' to reacquaint the very connection between their unlimited minds and bodies, which can be better understood when considered in light of Shahrazad's storytelling. In view of Cixous's assertion, I argue that the position Shahrazad possesses in story-telling is impressive since she does not only speak and tell stories, but is listened to attentively by the King and survives each night. In *Scheherazade Goes West*, Fatema Mernissi associates Shahrazad's survival with her intellect. She argues that '[Shahrazad] only survives because she is a super-strategist of the intellect. She would have been killed [if she] stretched out passively in the King's bed'.[55] Shahrazad is therefore a woman of intellect and strategy, who earns her survival through storytelling, which Malti-Douglas evaluates as Shahrazad's 'transition from sex to text'.[56] In contrast to Malti-Douglas, I argue that Shahrazad does not simply transition from the body to the text, but she incorporates her body into her narrative so intimately that it becomes impossible to consider them separate. She is able to reclaim the patriarchal literary discourse through which she makes 'the other language speak' with multiple narrators and characters.[57] This recla-mation is only possible when she exists within this storytelling with both her body and mind. Initially, Shahrazad is introduced to the narrative as a character. However, she evolves to become the legendary storyteller of the *Nights* because

---

53 As I aim not to contain Shahrazad's storytelling in narrative boundaries of an epilogue, I deliberately do not include Edgar Allan Poe's rather unfortunate ending for Shahrazad. Poe claims that the king would decapitate Shahrazad based on the preposterousness of her tales on the 1002nd night. In doing so, he completely ignores her mastery of storytelling and the fact that Shahrazad is aware of the risks she takes with every new tale. Poe's 'epilogue' is another way of Western 'mutilation' of Shahrazad's storytelling that I discuss in relation to Western translations of the tales. I argue for the potential of the 1002nd night (pp. 31–2) and successive nights because Shahrazad's narrative is constantly repeated in contemporary contexts and thus she never stops storytelling.

54 Cixous, 'Medusa', p. 887.

55 Fatema Mernissi, *Scheherazade Goes West: Different Cultures, Different Harems* (Washington Square Press: New York, 2001), p. 48.

56 Fedwa Malti-Douglas, *Woman's Body, Woman's Word: Gender and Discourse in Arabo-Islamic Writing* (Princeton, NJ: Princeton UP, 1991), p. 23.

57 Cixous, 'Medusa', p. 889.

she uses her body as a way to get inside the literary discourse and manipulate it 'from within' with a repetitive and endless cycle of narrative. Therefore, I would agree with Somaya Sami Sabry that '[Shahrazad] is best described as a manipulator of narrative desire, without fulfilling or satisfying the need for resolution.'[58] Hence, Shahrazad is not only heard; she also becomes liberated and a liberating figure with the reclamation/theft of the literary discourse.

Indeed, Cixous could be describing Shahrazad when she depicts the characteristics of a speaking woman: '[s]he must be farsighted [;] she foresees that her liberation will do more than modify power relations [...]; she will bring about a mutation in human relations',[59] because Shahrazad always thinks far ahead and constructs her stories with a clear intent to maintain the position of the storyteller.[60] Shahrazad structures her narrative to coincide the climax of the tale with the following dawn, so that it still requires resolution and captivates the attention of the audience, thus allowing her to live another day to finish the tale the following night. She has to be farsighted because she risks being decapitated while offering her body for the King's bed. The effects of her storytelling are immense: while narrating stories and occupying the King in her web of narration, she changes the personality of the King, a serial murderer, and liberates her cohort. The position of Shahrazad as a storyteller allows her to advise and educate the King on psychological, sociological and political matters as well as entertain him with her body and imagination. Shahrazad demonstrates that this form of storytelling is powerful and has the ability to modify power dynamics.[61] Subsequently, she not only discovers her own voice, but also acquires the position of 'a spokeswoman for the multifaceted intelligence and limitless abilities of women' when she addresses the King directly from within his bed.[62] Through

58 Somaya Sami Sabry, *Arab-American Women's Writing and Performance: Orientalism, Race and the Idea of The Arabian Nights* (I.B. Tauris: New York, 2011), p. 47.
59 Cixous, 'Medusa', p. 882.
60 Characters are carefully planned in each tale so much so that the King becomes a character of his own story being narrated to him as a part of the narrative chain. This not only reflects on Shahrazad's pre-planning of her stories, but it also shows her intellect by depicting characters in the third person.
61 Melissa Matthes points out that the King's regime is changed forever when he recommends his brother to marry Shahrazad's sister and share his throne with him. This suggests that Shahrazad eliminates his political 'despotism' and he agrees to share his power. Melissa Matthes, 'Shahrazad's Sisters: Storytelling and Politics in the Memoirs of Mernissi, el Saadawi and Ashrawi', *Alif*, 19 (1999), pp. 68–96, p. 71.
62 Suzanne Gauch, *Liberating Shahrazad: Feminism, Postcolonialism and Islam* (Minneapolis, MN: The University of Minnesota Press, 2007), p. x.

multiple narrators and perspectives, Shahrazad permits 'the language of 1000 tongues which knows neither enclosure nor death' to speak.[63] Moreover, because the storytelling takes place in the King's bedchamber, his safe place, he is more exposed to Shahrazad's skilful manipulation of his fixation with women's infidelity.[64] Shahrazad sexually manipulates the King to gain access to the position of the storyteller. However, Shahrazad simply differs from the King's previous sexual partners precisely because she also employs the power of her voice in this manipulation; thus postponing her execution nightly. Shahrazad is able to get within, both physically and mentally, and transform the patriarchal discourse with a form of narration that 'makes possible' her position in the patriarchal literary discourse.

In reviving Shahrazad's storytelling in their novels, Shafak and al-Shaykh are performing a political act, one which these contemporary postcolonial women writers repeat continuously. Until recently, Shahrazad had been restricted within a pre-defined colonial space. Muhsin Jassim al-Musawi points out that 'there is no trope that can accommodate the colonial desire better than the enormous taste for *The One Thousand and One Nights*'.[65] After their introduction to the West in the early eighteenth century, with Jean Antoine Galland's 'discovery', the *Nights* have been used as a text to enforce a binary distinction between the East and the West. The *Nights* became very popular with a Western readership, so much so that they were adopted and re-translated by multiple European travellers and Orientalists such as Richard Burton and Edward Lane. Confirming al-Musawi's claim, Suzanne Gauch suggests that these Western translations aimed to validate their understanding of the East and indicated their authority over the Orient. Indeed, Jorge Luis Borges explains how early European translators appropriated the *Nights* and aimed to present the text as 'a literal and complete' work of

---

63 Cixous, 'Medusa', p. 889.

64 Shahrazad re-tells the story of the adulterous queen from multiple perspectives and demonstrates how women are restricted within domestic boundaries and cheat in order to manipulate their situations from within these boundaries. One of these repeated tales shows how the king and his brother encounter a woman who is confined in a chest by a demon, cheats on the demon with both brothers. This does not only replicate the reasons of the Queen's infidelity, but also shifts the power dynamics by changing the position of the King from 'being cheated on' to 'being cheated with'. This tale is analysed in Chapter I.

65 Muhsin Jassim al-Musawi, *The Postcolonial Arabic Novel: Debating Ambivalence* (Leiden: Brill, 2003), p. 72.

literature.[66] In order to offer a definitive sense to the tales, the original of which were incomplete 'breaking off midstory after some 270 or so nights', Galland sought out different tales from various sources in the so-called Orient.[67] Borges argues, 'Galland established the canon, incorporating stories that time would render indispensable and [subsequent translators] would not dare omit'.[68] Borges demonstrates how Galland and other translators extend Shahrazad's silence by restricting her voice in pre-defined narrative boundaries. For instance, Galland and other translators include an epilogue that shows how Shahrazad is forgiven by the king and ceases storytelling to become a mother and wife. This epilogue was included in the translations to give the *Nights* a sense of finality and order. This is significant because the narrative cycle assumes an end when the thousand and first night comes and Shahrazad abandons storytelling. She is no longer a spokesperson who changes the course of a government with the repetition of her voice and silence. Rather, she is forced into a position of imposed silence if the tales are imagined as a definitive and complete work.

Shahrazad holds a significant but limited space until she is reclaimed by con-temporary postcolonial writers through literature. I therefore suggest that these Western translations reiterated the 'Oriental' woman's image, which included eventually rendering them voiceless and powerless. In doing so, the Western translators 'mutilated' Shahrazad by 'purifying' her tales through destruction.[69] Furthermore, they damaged Shahrazad's storytelling by losing gender differences in translation. For example, Borges suggests Lane 'purified' his translation and erased the image of a hermaphrodite fish by translating it as 'mixed species'. Most of the queer content has not been translated because it was 'bad taste [and] *too coarse for translation*'.[70] Galland and the subsequent translators aimed to create a linear and ordered version of the text and enforced a definitive epilogue. Thus, they restrained Shahrazad's ability to transgress boundaries and rejected the potentials of an open ending as well as of diverse subjectivities and sexualities. In contrast, postcolonial feminine writing imagines the possibility of the 1002nd night and subsequent nights by constantly reclaiming Shahrazad's voice because this implicitly refuses the structural and thematic boundaries imposed on the

---

66 Jorge Louis Borges, 'The Translators of the Thousand and One Nights', in *The Translation Studies Reader*, ed. By Lawrence Venuti (London and New York: Routledge, 2000), pp. 34–48, p. 42.

67 Gauch, *Liberating Shahrazad*, p. x.

68 Borges, 'Translators', p. 34.

69 Borges, 'Translators', p. 36.

70 Ibid., p. 36, emphasis in original.

Nights by the translations.[71] Shahrazad's contemporary re-narratives are postcolonial precisely because they indeed respond to Orientalist versions of the *Nights*. The return to the voice of a tenth century Eastern storyteller is also a form of feminine writing:[72] '[h]ere they are, returning, arriving over and again, because the unconscious is impregnable. They have wandered around in circles, confined to the narrow room in which they've been given a deadly brainwashing.'[73] Here, it is imperative to return and arrive at a position of narrative that revives the woman's body within narrative because in doing so contemporary postcolonial women writers transcend the previous positions offered to Shahrazad in how they deal with restrictions on women.

Although the *Nights* has been presented as 'a monolithic embodiment' of a very diverse group of people, new and progressive understandings and re-imaginings of Shahrazad tend to undermine the previous confinement.[74] For example, Suzanne Gauch addresses how Shahrazad's challenge is reformed and made twofold in these re-imaginings: 'to combat symbolic and political violence at home and to struggle against co-option by imperialist or anti-Islamic critics abroad.'[75] Gauch analyses several works that follow a Shahrazadean tradition to demonstrate Shahrazad 'as a speaking agent whose stories have never ended and whose resolve has only increased in the face of both rising fundamentalisms and proliferating Western media images of Arab and Muslim women as silent, oppressed, exploited, and uneducated victims.'[76] In doing so, Gauch offers insight into the re-positioning of Shahrazad in the discourses of 'the Occident and the Orient'. Hence, she elicits Shahrazad as an infinite narrator, who should not be narrowed to a definitive image or discourse, and whose tales are timelessly

---

71 'One Thousand and One', ('*binbir*' in Turkish, '*Alf Layla wa-Layla*' in Arabic), connotes infinity and endlessness in both Turkish and Arabic rather than simply referring to a number, which is largely lost in translation. See Somaya Sami Sabry, 'Performing Sheherazade: Arab-American Women's Contestations of Identity', *Alif: Journal of Comparative Poetics*, 31 (2011), pp. 196–219, p. 196.
72 Gauch considers a tenth century catalogue of books, the *Kitab al-Fihrist* of Ibn al-Nadim, the earliest reference to Shahrazad. *Liberating Shahrazad*, p. x.
73 Cixous, 'Medusa', p. 877.
74 Sabry, *Arab-American Women's Writing*, p. 23.
75 Gauch, *Liberating Shahrazad*, p. xi. Gauch's discussion of 'Shahrazad's challenge' is based on Mernissi's *Scheherazade Goes West*, which provides Mernissi's semi-autobiographical and semi-fictional accounts of her experiences in the West while promoting her book. She makes several observations on the allure of Shahrazad as an Oriental symbol and the Western harems confining women to body image and beauty ideals.
76 Ibid., p. xi.

resistant to oppressions both at home and abroad. Gauch argues that 'Shahrazad is no political radical; the changes at which her storytelling ultimately aims are not violent. Rather, her stories bit by bit overcome what were once seemingly insurmountable boundaries'.[77] Similarly, I argue that Shahrazad deconstructs the dominant roles and hierarchies within her storytelling. Although she intervenes in the King's political affairs by narrating various instances of political government, she extends the changes over a period of time. This does not render her powerless; rather, Shahrazad is empowered because 'simply by making others listen, [she] is able to change the course of a government'.[78] Thus, I agree with Gauch that 'liberating should not be interpreted as an action to be performed on Shahrazad. [Rather,] liberating must be read as Shahrazad's distinguishing attribute'.[79] Recognising Shahrazad's self-liberation, I similarly suggest that Shahrazad is no victim on whom a liberating act is performed. Instead, liberating should be recognised as what she does by saving both herself and other women from the King's dominance.

While I demonstrate that Shahrazad is a powerful storyteller, whose voice subverts the patriarchal and literary discourses, I also want to emphasise that Shahrazad was also previously recognised simply as an Oriental figure. As I discussed earlier, Shahrazad's voice and narrative are limited in Western translations. These translations accommodate Shahrazad's storytelling to present an understanding and image of the Orient. It is worth turning to Edward Said here, who defines Orientalism with regard to the power dynamics between the West and the East. In Orientalism, Said posits that the West is defined in a constant hierarchy over the East suggesting an inherent superiority of the West over the East.[80] The Orient simply becomes an object to be confined and analysed. Anastasia Valassopoulos argues that contemporary postcolonial women writers re-exoticize the Orient by focusing on Orientalist arts such as paintings and travel writing. She argues for the possibility of a mobile version of Orientalism that keeps changing. Valassopoulos suggests that this is 'a particular postcolonial requisitioning of the past' since it complicates not only the present but suggests new imaginings of the past that is considered static – while Orientalism is central to these contemporary re-narratives, the latter also subverts and transforms it.[81]

---

77 Gauch, Liberating Shahrazad, p. xviii.
78 Ibid., p. 134.
79 Ibid., p. xviii.
80 Edward W. Said, Orientalism (London and New York: Penguin, 2003), p. 7.
81 Valassopoulos, Contemporary Arab Women Writers, p. 144.

This contemporary analysis of Orientalism indicates that a new form of resistance to the idea of a uniformed past is present in contemporary postcolonial women's writing as it operates on a level that is not restricted to a pre-defined time frame. I argue that contemporary women writers develop an interrogation of how Orientalist practices exploit Shahrazad's storytelling to have 'an overwhelming [...] knowledge about the Orient'.[82] Contemporary re-imaginings of Shahrazad rework this Oriental image and subvert it from a perspective that is different from the oriental, which simply leaves Shahrazad silenced and subordinate. They do not fail to be more than resistant as they fight the orientalist imagery in ways that undo both past and present. Precisely because they construct and deconstruct the links between the colonial past and the postcolonial present by using texts employed by Orientalists, they refuse the clear-cut historical narration of colonialism and Orientalism.

More importantly for *Postcolonial Feminine Writing*, the conception of the East as inferior depends on and is defined by the position of non-Western women's bodies. They prove to be national and racial boundary markers and provide the excuse for continuing oriental and neo-imperial expeditions.[83] Fedwa Malti-Douglas aptly states that non-Western women and their roles are reduced to being 'a stick with which the West can beat the East'.[84] Therefore it is significant to incorporate the bodies of non-Western women into postcolonial feminine writing because it responds to colonial and neo-colonial narratives in ways that have been neglected and that re-define their boundaries and differences, but with themselves as the subject, not as the object to be investigated. Postcolonial feminine writing offers an insight into these women's bodily experiences in a way that does not simply set them apart or define them in a hierarchy. It does not mean that these writers expect to provide an insider's insight intended specifically for the Western reader. On the contrary, contemporary postcolonial women writers use English, the language that surrounds them with boundaries, in order

---

82 Ibid., p. 140.

83 Katherine Viner reported that Bush bombed Afghanistan to liberate Afghan women from their burqas. Katherine Viner, 'Feminism as Imperialism', *The Guardian*, 21st September 2002, <http://www.theguardian.com/world/2002/sep/21/gender.usa> [accessed 20 August 2019]. Furthermore, the Western media and politics continue to centralise non-Western women's bodies in their reprehension of the East. For example, Lauren Bohn, ' "We're All Handcuffed in This Country." Why Afghanistan Is Still the Worst Place in the World to Be a Woman', *TIME*, 8 December 2018, <https://time.com/5472411/afghanistan-women-justice-war/> [accessed 20 August 2019].

84 Malti-Douglas, *Woman's Body, Woman's Word*, p. 3.

to break down the constructed images around their own bodies. Accordingly, I focus on the links between Cixous, Fanon and Shahrazad to draw out a theoretical frame for this concept.

The Theoretical Frame of Postcolonial Feminine Writing

In 'Sorties', Hélène Cixous discusses how women are almost always restricted within a binary opposition in patriarchal discourse. She argues that women are left in a position of passivity or death in a pre-defined hierarchy because '[o]rganization by hierarchy makes all conceptual organizations subject to man. Male privilege [is] shown in the opposition between *activity* and *passivity*. [In this hierarchy,] woman is passive or she does not exist. What is left of her is unthinkable, unthought'.[85] The patriarchal discourse almost always assumes male privilege as superior and produces the binary opposition that recognises women's existence as simply the inferior other. This suggests that women are not only oppressed by this hierarchy, but their existences are also left 'unthought' and unexplored. I argue that women's voices refuse to stay within this binary that 'unthinks' their existences because their bodily experiences are different and not containable. Cixous suggests that it is impossible for women to stay in the position they are oppressed into because 'you can't talk about *a* female sexuality, uniform, homogeneous, classifiable into codes'.[86] Here, female sexuality is not simply a reversal or binary opposite to male sexuality. It is not defined by or limited to the codes that classify masculinity. This suggest that female sexuality, which Cixous addresses, has the potential to transform the interpretation of these codes.

In the 'Laugh of Medusa', Cixous re-interprets how these codes distanced women from their bodies and writing. She proclaims that women should write themselves so that their bodies can 'be heard. Only then the immense resources of the unconscious spring forth'.[87] Therefore, women must revive their connection with their bodies, and only after that will they 'seize[…] the occasion to speak'.[88] She indicates that women's speech is a paradox and 'how great a transgression it

---

85 Hélène Cixous, 'Sorties: Out and Out: Attacks/Ways Out/Forays' (originally published in Paris as *La Jeune Née*, 1975), in *The Newly Born Woman*, ed. By Hélène Cixous and Catherine Clément, trans. By Betsy Wing (Manchester: Manchester University Press, 1986), pp. 37–9. Emphasis in original.

86 Cixous, 'Medusa', p. 876, emphasis in original.

87 Ibid., p. 880.

88 Ibid., p. 880.

is for a woman to speak [since] her words fall almost always upon the deaf male ear.'[89] Cixous declares that women embody the (im)possibility of speech. For that matter, the very possibility of women's speech requires that women understand the 'immense resources' that their bodies possess and embrace them to create the opportunity of speech. In this sense, women are expected to 'transgress' the limiting patriarchal discourse to speak:

> Her writing can only keep going, without ever inscribing or discerning contours [...]. She alone dares and wishes to know from within, where she, the outcast, has never ceased to hear the resonance of fore-language. She lets the other language speak – the language of 1000 tongues which knows neither enclosure nor death. [...] Her language does not contain, it carries; it does not hold back, it makes possible.[90]

While the patriarchal discourse tends to restrict women within a binary opposition that immediately erases their voices, Cixous 'dares and wishes' to demonstrate that feminine writing exists, and it is not recognised by the patriarchal discourse because it is not limited by the same 'contours'. This is a potentially strong position because it effectively disregards the position of women's passivity by recognising the feminine that is defined not by the patriarchal authority, but their own bodies. Here, I want to point out that the notion of the feminine is not simply biologically determined, specifically because Cixous aims to break down restrictive binary oppositions, demonstrating how some male authors also apply feminine writing in their texts. For instance, Susan Sellers argues that 'there is a deliberate complicating of biological determinism [in 'Medusa']. Cixous is careful to avoid any fetishizing notion of an ideal female body; rather, the essay celebrates the plurality of women's different bodies'.[91] Cixous's position in recognising, and moreover celebrating, the plurality of bodies complicates the positionality of the woman's body within a binary structure.

Cixous argues for an impossibility of controlling feminine writing because it does not simply have defined boundaries. In 'Medusa', she focuses on the difference of feminine forms of writing:

> It is impossible to define a feminine practice of writing and this is an impossibility that will remain, for this practice can never be theorized, enclosed, coded – which doesn't mean that it doesn't exist. But it will always surpass the discourse that regulates the phallocentric system; it does and will take place in areas other than those subordinated

---

89 Ibid., p. 881.
90 Ibid., p. 889.
91 Susan Sellers, 'On Hélène Cixous's "The Laugh of Medusa"', *Women: A Cultural Review*, 21, 1 (2010), pp. 22–5, p. 24.

to philosophico-theoretical domination. It will be conceived of only by subjects who are breakers of automatisms, by peripheral figures that no authority can ever subjugate.[92]

Feminine writing refuses to be 'enclosed' in the same manner as masculine forms of writing. Therefore, it is difficult to trace feminine writing with the same language and literary discourse as its masculine equivalent. However, this does not suggest that a very feminine form of writing does not exist simply because it does not stay within the same parameters. It 'surpasses' the patriarchal systems of language and thus can only be accomplished by 'breakers of automatisms'. She posits the idea of femininity within writing whereby '[w]oman must write her self: must write about women and bring women to writing, from which they have been driven away as violently as from their bodies'.[93] Therefore, writing is *the very possibility of change, the space that can serve as a springboard for sub-versive thought'.[94]* The potential of feminine writing shall be 'without contours' and formulated as a position of language that carries the language forward. This form of writing can be explored as breaking the boundaries of male-dom-inated patriarchal literary discourse by stealing it and breaking these norms 'from within'. Ann Rosalind Jones explains how feminine writing can transgress the boundaries of the patriarchal discourse by tracing formal qualities such as 'double or multiple voices, broken syntax, repetitive or cumulative rather than linear structure, [and] open endings'.[95] This book demonstrates that these forms of narrative are re-enacted in contemporary postcolonial women's writing by mimicking Shahrazad's storytelling in constructing multiple voices/narrators, repetitive and non-linear storylines and open-ended stories. Postcolonial femi-nine writing helps us to understand how the repetition of these styles is a delib-erate intervention in the patriarchal literary discourse and reinvents women's voices in the literary context.

Almost a 'photographic negative' to Cixous's collection of interviews, *White Ink*, Shafak's semi-autobiographical *Black Milk* offers a creative and theoretical analysis of feminine writing by focusing on motherhood, creativity and story-telling.[96] As explored by Claire Chambers, both expressions bring to mind a link

---

92 Cixous, 'Medusa', p. 883.
93 Cixous, 'Medusa', p. 875.
94 Ibid., p. 879.
95 Ann Rosalind Jones, 'Inscribing femininity: French theories of the feminine', in *Making A Difference: Feminist Literary Criticism*, ed. By Gayle Green and Coppelia Kahn (London: Routledge, 1985), pp.80–112, p. 88.
96 Claire Chambers, *Rivers of Ink: Selected Essays* (Karachi: Oxford UP, 2017), p. xxii.

between breast milk and *l'écriture feminine*.[97] However, *Black Milk* stands both as an example of and complicating feminine writing. Shafak inverts Cixous's term by reconfiguring milk as 'black' and not as pure as Cixous implies. Whilst *White Ink* gives an essentialist sense of breast milk as though dripping onto page and becoming the source of creativity for women, *Black Milk* offers a confrontational experience of women's creativity, which does not simply descend from motherhood and breastmilk, but presents a nuanced understanding of women's writing. Moreover, by inverting this expression, *Black Milk* re-contextualises Cixous's *l'écriture feminine* in a way that is also relevant to both contemporary readers and writers of colour. As *Black Milk* engages with the links between motherhood and writing, Shafak also reflects on her postpartum depression, abandonment of writing and her eventual return to storytelling supported by her new role as a mother. Despite potentially following a form of feminine writing, this reversal of the term also attempts to problematise the understanding of feminine writing as essentialist. Specifically because *Black Milk* draws on examples of various women writers, some of whom are not mothers or those who abandoned motherhood for writing, it does not signify breast milk as central to women's writing. I would therefore suggest that Shafak does not simply bring her or women's bodies back to writing. Rather, *Black Milk* demonstrates how bodies are already in writing and offers an embodied conception of writing. Throughout the book, Shafak reflects on how she silences several aspects of her femininity and motherhood as evidenced by 'the manifesto of the single girl'.[98] This manifesto renounces traditional views on women and motherhood and thus guides Shafak 'to make a choice between uterus and brain' as dictated by leading male novelists in Turkey.[99]

Similar to Cixous's 'Sorties', *Black Milk* interrogates several binary oppositions and opens the binary oppositions of 'man/woman, masculine/feminine, bold/modest, dominant/passive [...]' up for a new interrogation into what is a natural/cultural construct.[100] Through critical and occasionally poetical interrogations of similar binary oppositions, *Black Milk* reveals how 'female writers can't write about sexuality as freely as male writers do'.[101] By distancing from writing about sexuality, women writers are similarly distanced and alienated from their bodies.

97   Ibid., p. xxii.
98   Elif Shafak, *Black Milk: On the Conflicting Demands of Writing, Creativity, and Motherhood*, trans. By Hande Zapsu (London: Penguin, 2007), p. 17.
99   Ibid., p. 19.
100 Ibid., p. 129.
101 Ibid., p. 159.

Moreover, *Black Milk* shows how several women writers who adopted androgynous or male pseudonym as 'an armor to shield [themselves] need the protection even more when [they] write about sexuality, femininity and the body. [W]orrying about the permission to tell the story – be it personal or familial – is particular to women writers all around the world'.[102] In order to transcend this restricted position, Shafak offers her own experience of pregnancy and motherhood as a source of new imaginary practices. To an extent, breast milk figuratively presents the source for a feminine practice of writing that Cixous asserts as never 'theorized, enclosed [or] coded' just as breast milk itself transcends patriarchal dichotomies.[103] Black in *Black Milk* suggests that it is not the real, but the metaphorical use of breast milk that offers a subversion of social and gender norms. Alison Bartlett suggests that breastfeeding is a performative act and it is the repeatedness of breastfeeding that gives an illusion of successful motherhood.[104] The success of motherhood based on breastfeeding is defined by patriarchal norms and confines women to a limited space. Similar to my conception of (un)veiling, *Black Milk* does not conform to societal and patriarchal limitations, when it is most expected to conform, by transferring the understanding of breast milk from real to metaphorical on page. It is subversive of patriarchal norms of motherhood because it makes the breast milk, which was once familiar and recognisable in a patriarchal context, unfamiliar and unrecognisable as 'black'. Therefore, it offers an embodied sense of creativity, but it also queers the act of breastfeeding by giving it a metaphorical standpoint. Thus, *Black Milk* transcends the limited patriarchal understanding of breast milk and allows different others the potential to go beyond these limitations.

Cixous argues that flying in language and making language fly is a 'woman's gesture'.[105] This is because '[women] have all learned the art of flying, [...] been able to possess anything only by flying, [...] stealing away, finding [...] hidden crossovers'.[106] Here, flight is associated with freedom and boundlessness. While women stay connected to their bodies, they fly to avoid being restrained.

---

102 Ibid., p. 101. Here, Shafak may ignore local differences women writers encounter in their writing process in favour of global sisterhood. While it can be considered as a problem at face value, Shafak does not maintain this undermining of local differences in her novels.

103 Cixous, 'Medusa', p. 883.

104 Alison Bartlett, 'Thinking through Breasts: Writing Maternity', *Feminist Theory*, 1, 2 (2000), pp. 173–88, p. 179.

105 Cixous, 'Medusa', p. 887.

106 Ibid., p. 887.

Fatema Mernissi relates to 'flight' in her autobiography by remembering her grandmother's advice, ' "[w]hen a woman decides to use her wings, she takes big risks", [however], when a woman doesn't use her wings at all, it hurts her'.[107] Thus, 'using wings' is a big risk to take for a woman because she transgresses boundaries that restrict her.[108] Nonetheless, Mernissi recounts it as a necessary action; otherwise, women remain helpless victims who are subject to physical or emotional violence. I would argue that Shahrazad is also in flight when she acquires the power of storytelling. She makes a claim to the level that is supposed to be forbidden to women. Shahrazad breaks down binary structures and reveals them to be dislocated. She uses the means of storytelling to 'disorient' the narrative discourse she inherits. Storytelling is liberated from the mainstream authority in a non-linear and everlasting structure by Shahrazad. Therefore, the logic of feminine writing has long existed in a non-Western context through the figure of Shahrazad. This contradicts the view of non-Western women as victims and the idea that feminism is a Western concept. For instance, Mernissi suggests that the position of the storyteller 'as a symbol of human rights' has existed with Shahrazad while the Arab conservative male elite 'for centuries [...] scorned [the Nights] as popular trash of no cultural value whatsoever, because the tales were transmitted orally'.[109] Mernissi poses the question, was the reason behind this censure 'because the tales were mostly narrated by women within the private realm of the family?'.[110] Although there is no conclusive research focused on this perception, along similar lines al-Musawi argues that the trope of Shahrazad is 'feminized [and] equated with the female body, to be secretly searched for, but veiled from the public eye or openly disdained and ostracized as a paradigm of evil'.[111] Therefore, Shahrazad has held a significant position of ' "feminine" [in] very "masculine" Muslim heritage'.[112] Postcolonial feminine writing therefore both revisits and further develops this logic of feminine writing in a postcolonial context.

The concept of postcolonial feminine writing builds on this Cixousian perspective of feminine writing and Shahrazad's storytelling, along with Fanon's discussion of (un)veiling. It is not only a refusal to be restricted within boundaries of patriarchal thought and linearity, but an urge to work within these

---

107 Mernisi, *Scheherazade*, pp. 3–4.
108 This concept of flight will specifically be explored in Chapter II, p. 88 and p. 102.
109 Mernissi, *Scheherazade*, p. 55.
110 Ibid., p. 55.
111 Al-Musawi, *The Postcolonial Arabic Novel*, p. 77.
112 Mernissi, *Scheherazade*, p. 55.

boundaries to liberate the literary discourse from within. In order to re-interpret the discourse of the veil and (un)veiling, I draw extensively on Frantz Fanon's 'Algeria Unveiled' because it demonstrates how non-Western women are able to re-define their identities by employing the veil against colonial and patriarchal conventions. I suggest that the process of (un)veiling is a multifaceted discourse that has not been considered in its entirety by critics thus far. For example, Marie-Aimee Helie-Lucas states that having women freedom fighters in the war did not just abolish gender distinctions. While a man is called 'fighter', a woman is called 'a helper'.[113] Helie-Lucas critiques Fanon mainly because his praising the revolutionary virtue of the veil prevents the veil from being re-presented as oppressive 'without betraying both the nation and the revolution'.[114] However, she does not recognise Fanon's ideal of resisting colonialism alongside the colonial desire to unveil the Algerian woman. The idea was to 'conquer' Algerian women's bodies with European ideals as a colonial technique, which in turn would provide the transformation of Algerian society. Fanon reads this 'unveiling' desire as 'double flowering', both a physical and a symbolic penetration of Algerian society.[115] Thereby, the protection from colonialism initially necessitated the protection from this 'double flowering'. Likewise, Diana Fuss criticises 'Algeria Unveiled', because of the text's utilisation of the veil leads to the 'exclusion of the women from the public sphere'.[116] It seems that Fuss's primary focus on the veil as a religious symbol ostensibly neglects the significance of the repetitiveness of (un)veiling in Algerian women's involvement in liberation.

In contrast to these arguments, I suggest that (un)veiling is a performative act that transforms the ways in which non-Western women's bodies are produced, since it both reconnects their bodies to their voices and also transforms gender and national boundaries. The veil is meant to construct a binary opposition between non-Western women and men and also non-Western and Western societies. Fanon argues that it is with 'the outbreak of the struggle for liberation' that the fate of Algerian women dramatically changes.[117] He recognises the

---

113 Marie-Aimee Helie Lucas, 'Women, Nationalism and Religion in the Algerian Liberation Struggle', in *Rethinking Fanon*, ed. by Nigel Gibson (New York: Humanity Books, 1999), pp. 271–82, p. 272.

114 Ibid., p. 275.

115 Frantz Fanon, 'Algeria Unveiled', in *A Dying Colonialism*, trans. by Haakon Chevalier (New York: Grove Press, 1959, 1965), pp. 35–68, p. 45.

116 Diana Fuss, 'Interior Colonies: Frantz Fanon and the Politics of Identification', in *Rethinking Fanon*, ed. by Nigel Gibson (New York: Humanity Books, 1999), pp. 294–328, p. 304.

117 Fanon, 'Algeria Unveiled', p. 47.

active participation of women in the liberation battle as 'a revolutionary step'. Algerian women are re-acquainted with their roles as 'women alone in the street' and the revolutionary mission. Thus, (un)veiling is a gendered and racialized act manifested in non-Western women's search for liberation because '[w]hat the colonial gaze saw in the Algerian women's disturbing mimicry was a displacement of its own representation of the veil. Hence what once was familiar and recognizable as concealment, mask, masquerading, has now become unfamiliar [and] disturbing'.[118] Here, the veil is not simply a demonstration of religiosity. It is re-enacted as a reformed practice that deflects the colonial disregard of the veil. Even though the veil seems to offer a definitive idea of non-Western women for the colonisers, it is also meant to 'prevent the colonial gaze from attaining such a visibility and hence mastery' over non-Western women.[119] Fanon reflects how the colonising mission was dependent on 'converting the woman, winning her over to the foreign values, wrenching her free from her [inferior] status'.[120] Therefore, for colonisers, unveiling Algeria meant unveiling 'Algerian society whose systems of defense were in the process of dislocation' and integrating European values into this dislocated society.[121] Non-Western women's bodies were battlegrounds for colonial Algeria, but Algerian women resisted this colonial act and manipulated the means that were used to restrain them. Gradually, Algerian women gain control of their bodies as they (un)veil to appear as if they were conforming to European values: 'Removed and reassumed again and again, the veil has been manipulated, transformed into a technique of camouflage, into a means of struggle'.[122] This notion of (un)veiling does not simply incorporate gender norms in a transforming national context. Rather, it is the process of repetition involved in this act of (un)veiling that is subversive and allows for these social and national transformations. The veil is not merely a boundary marker in gender and national contexts. Through this repeated subversion of the meaning of the veil it becomes a form of camouflage which allows women to transcend the boundaries that assumed their conformity. It is because they (un)veiled in order to seemingly conform to their conditions that they could subvert the image of a non-Western woman. What makes this act of (un)veiling both resistant and powerful is how this act is re-defining and re-defined by non-Western women's

---

118 Meyda Yeğenoğlu, *Colonial Fantasies: Towards a Feminist Reading of Orientalism* (Cambridge: Cambridge UP, 1998), p. 65.
119 Ibid., p. 12.
120 Fanon, 'Algeria Unveiled', p. 39.
121 Ibid., p. 42.
122 Ibid., p. 61.

bodies. They employ the veil as a symbol of resistance, because it inherently belongs to them. However, (un)veiling is not merely a process of taking off the veil for my analysis of postcolonial feminine writing.

The veil is not simply a piece of cloth or a religious symbol in 'Algeria Unveiled', (un)veiling is both the symbolic and literal undoing of power because colonial power dynamics are open to manipulation. Therefore, I re-formulate the process of (un)veiling as a gender non-conforming act which postcolonial feminine writing adopts in various ways. (Un)veiling gives the power to non-Western women by allowing them to subvert colonial and gendered assumptions over their bodies and enables them to control how their bodies are defined. By seeming to conform, non-Western women gain the authority to transgress social and gender boundaries. Here, literature/writing becomes a significant means of communication in how social norms are enacted and may be re-enacted. I ana-lyse (un)veiling as a form of gender non-conforming disguise in my literary chapters as several narrators and characters use different forms of disguise in the selected novels. Therefore, I suggest (un)veiling also unveils how the process of repetition in women's writing results in an undoing of the social norms that attempts to 'unthink' women's existences. It becomes a technique for contem-porary women writers to assume different voices through different narrators. It gives authors the potential of a disguise, or camouflage as Fanon would put it, to deflect the gaze as well as the chance to reform social and gender norms as evidenced by Fanon's essay itself. I would argue that writing is a significant aspect of reclaiming and re-forming social norms inasmuch as Fanon reclaims Algerian history and the revolution story by writing 'Algeria Unveiled'.

The differences in the French and English titles of Fanon's book also show how Fanon considers writing as a significant medium in revolution. The collec-tion of essays, including 'Algeria Unveiled', that has been translated into English as *A Dying Colonialism* is titled *L'an Cinq, de la Revolution Algerienne*, which means 'the fifth year of Algerian revolution'.[123] This suggests that Fanon reclaims the history of Algerian national liberation, which during French colonial rule has been written from the perspective of French history, by defining the mo-ment of Algerian revolution in time (the fifth year). Fanon re-writes his own story of decolonisation by re-writing Algerian history. Thus, Fanon is not simply a history-maker or a postcolonial theorist, but he is also the storyteller of this

---

123 Donna McCormack, 'Gender and Colonial Transitioning: Frantz Fanon's Algerian Freedom Fighters in Moroccan and Caribbean Novels?', *Journal of Transatlantic Studies*, 7, 3 (2009), pp. 279–93, p. 279.

revolution story. This reclamation shows significant transformation in gender norms, which is evidenced through changing family values and women's active involvement in national liberation.[124] I therefore suggest this indicates the importance of re-claiming narration of one's own story in decolonising social and gender norms. Here, Fanon becomes a symbolic Shahrazad in subverting the French story and re-writing the Algerian version of the same story.

(Un)veiling Shahrazad

Here, I want to take a close look at how other critics engage with similar themes in order to situate my argument in a broader context of postcolonial literature and demonstrate the difference of my own criticism. I suggest that the novels analysed in this book mirror Shahrazad's narrative in many ways, but also transcend it because they offer a new response to both colonial, neo-colonial and patriarchal attempts at controlling non-Western women. Al-Musawi considers Shahrazad's narrative in a postcolonial context as a decolonisation of the patriarchal literary discourse: '[l]iberating herself and women at large from control, this very Scheherazade [in contemporary literary works] is a decolonizing trope, too, as the significations of liberation narrative resonate with reference to women in their material reality or as symbols of the *ummah* or the nation in its fight against the colonizer'.[125] This suggests and confirms Gauch's argument that Shahrazad's 'challenge' works on multiple levels.[126] The re-writings of Shahrazad therefore point out how she does not only defeat the image of 'Oriental' woman, and but also fights the image of woman within '*the ummah*'.[127] This shows how Shahrazad is a multifaceted narrator as well as a political figure and firmly situates her in the decolonising role in contemporary postcolonial women's writing, demonstrating how as a figure she may be deployed as a methodology that I am naming postcolonial feminine writing.

Having established my concept of postcolonial feminine writing at the intersections of postcolonialism, feminine writing and Shahrazad's storytelling, it is important to situate this approach in relation to existing literary criticism about non-Western women's writing. The representation of non-Western women in the West has gradually changed with more texts being translated into English and

---

124 Ibid., p. 280.
125 Al-Musawi, *The Postcolonial Arabic Novel*, p. 15.
126 Gauch, *Liberating Shahrazad*, p. xi.
127 Al-Musawi, p. 15.

other European languages towards the end of the twentieth century. However, this also sheds light on the politics of translation in terms of how authors and texts have been translated selectively. For instance, Amal Amireh and Lisa Suhair Majaj question the transnational reception of Third World women's writing at the turn of this century. They claim that these texts are received by transnational contexts in a 'predefined space' that 'merely' reinforces 'what [their] audiences already "knew" – that is the patriarchal, oppressive nature of Third World societies'.[128] This suggests that non-Western women writers who have not openly criticised their nations and traditions are not heard at all. Consequently, non-Western women's texts were simply assumed to be ' "mediators" between East and West' and thus a source of 'cultural authenticity'.[129] The politics of translation largely limited the inclusion of non-Western women in the Western discourse and proved dangerous since it only maintained, instead of questioning and negotiating the 'power asymmetry' between the West and the East. Along similar lines, Lisa Suhair Majaj, Paula W. Sunderman and Therese Saliba focus on the need to situate Arab women's novels for an English-speaking readership. They point out that the Western discussion of Arab women suggests how 'Arab women are in need of being "saved" from their own cultures'.[130] Both critics indicate the limitations of the reception of non-Western women's texts and have set out specific and local issues addressed in these texts. Although they can be considered as pioneers in critiquing non-Western women's writings on more sympathetic lines, they have a limited focus mainly due to the availability of translations. While they particularly indicate tensions between gender and nation, they do not address the intersectionality of oppressions faced by non-Western women such as class and race. Therefore, I suggest literary criticism has sustained the impression of victimhood and failed to recognise the potential of subversion. It is also worth mentioning that the main focus of these critiques has been non-Western women's experiences and writings of war. In this context, Miriam Cooke discusses how women have been 'left out of history, out of the War story' although they have been part of the struggle.[131] Elsewhere, Cooke

---

128 Amal Amireh and Lisa Suhair Majaj, *Going Global: The Transnational Reception of the Third World Women Writers* (New York and London: Garland Publishing, 2000), p. 1.
129 Ibid., p. 2.
130 Lisa Suahir Majaj et al., *Intersections: Gender, Nation, and Community in Arab Women's Novels* (Syracuse, NY: Syracuse UP, 2002), p. xviii.
131 Miriam Cooke, *Women Claim Islam: Creating Islamic Feminism through Literature* (London and New York: Routledge, 2001), p. vii.

draws particular attention to how women conform within the army by cross-dressing.[132] Thus, it seems gender roles can become ambiguous during war, as also reflected in non-Western women's texts. While it is significant to bring non-Western women's 'out of history' voices into context, Cooke discusses that the ambiguity of gender roles could not be maintained afterwards. While literary criticism on war-writing proves to be a significant part of non-Western women's writing, little has been produced in relation to contemporary works of literature. Therefore, the focus of these critiques, while it remains valid and necessary, is rather narrow and centred on the colonial past.

A successful intervention in contemporary postcolonial literary criticism would be Claire Chambers's 'multi-sensory' approach to British Muslim novels. *Making Sense of Contemporary British Muslim Novels* challenges and complicates British Muslim identities on multiple levels as it undermines Islamophobic depictions of Muslims. Due to Chambers's acceptance of 1989 as a turning point for Islamophobia in the UK, following the Rushdie affair, she draws on several examples of British Muslim male and female writers to challenge the unified and homogenous Muslim/terrorist image. Moreover, she offers an innovative engagement with both postcolonial and sensory studies by drawing out the links between senses, and therefore destabilises stereotypes. That is, Chambers facilitates an 'intersensorality' experience of analysing postcolonial novels from a sensory perspective.[133] In doing so, she suggests the significance of the senses in understanding British Muslim fiction as senses stand for 'an act of protest'.[134] This resistance, Chambers indicates, does not simply 'reverse the gaze, [but it] lay stress on the other senses'.[135] Therefore, I would suggest that she 'braids together' all senses to unsettle the predominance of the (Oriental) gaze as well as to engage with multiple representations of (gendered, racialised and Muslim) bodies by providing 'full-bodied' experiences in British Muslim writing.[136] Furthermore,

---

132 Miriam Cooke, 'Arab Women, Arab Wars', *Cultural Critique*, 29 (1994–95), pp. 5–29, p. 15.

133 Chambers concentrates on different senses (touch, smell, taste and sound) in each chapter and argues how these senses are indeed not inferior to the sense of sight. For instance, Chambers draws attention to how touch manifests in Ahdaf Soueif's *In the Eye of the Sun* as a means of knowledge through the protagonist's sexualised body whereas she focuses on the sense of taste as a symbol of identity in Leila Aboulela's *Minaret*.

134 Claire Chambers, *Making Sense of Contemporary British Muslim Novels* (London: Palgrave Macmillan, 2019), p. xxxii.

135 Ibid., p. xxxii.

136 Ibid., p. xxii.

Chambers argues that this act of resistance is 'double-edged' as it both resists 'marginalization or cover-up of non-heteronormative sexualities and women's rights that sometimes occurs in Muslim communities, but also [...] successive British governments' attempts to surveil, control and suppress Muslim bodies'.[137] Similarly, I discuss how the reclamation of Shahrazad's storytelling by Shafak and al-Shaykh is 'double-edged' in resisting both domestic and Western restrictions. However, Chambers expresses her concern over excluding al-Shaykh and Shafak from her monograph, considering both writers can be identified as British Muslim writers. Hence, I aim to fill this gap by taking a close look at their novels in a transnational context with the figure of Shahrazad. Conversely, I do not engage with the religious identity of Shafak and al-Shaykh precisely because I want to specifically concentrate on their novels in the context of postcolonial feminine writing. As I have discussed earlier, they do not conform to Western expectations of 'Muslim women writers' producing 'informative [and] characteristic' stories of 'unhappy' Muslim women. Resultantly, I want to acknowledge that both writers exceed this context of 'Muslim' writers even though they come from Muslim backgrounds. In doing so, I aim to look at Shafak and al-Shaykh as both local and universal authors without reducing them to a religious or national category.

As a significant critique of postcolonial women's writing, Anastasia Valassopoulos offers a 'spirit of transcultural and transnational communication' by presenting an informed discussion of the contexts in which non-Western women's texts are considered. Valassopoulos expands the discussions surrounding Arab women writers by approaching their texts from multiple social and cultural perspectives. She brings together Arab women writers from different national backgrounds to argue that it should be possible to read Arab women writers 'not only in terms of the representation and self-representation of [themselves] but indeed across the spectrum of critical theory'.[138] This opens up the possibility of extending the discussion of Arab women's writings from a socio-cultural and religious perspectives to more of a literary representation. Correspondingly, Lindsey Moore focuses on Arab women writers' voices and vision presenting a wide contextual focus by critically engaging with multiple postcolonial, feminist, literary and cinematic perspectives. Both Valassopoulos and Moore endeavour to offer insight into both well-known and less-translated Arab women writers based on the availability of translations. They seek

137 Ibid., p. xxxii.
138 Valassopoulos, *Contemporary Arab Women Writers*, p. 27.

to construct a critical and transnational dialogue and a postcolonial consciousness by pointing out multiple intersections of power dynamics and reading non-Western women's writing without a 'patronizing admiration that Arab Muslim women write at all'.[139] I would therefore suggest non-Western women's writing has only recently been analysed in relation to literary theory more broadly and not yet in the context of feminine writing. An exemption to this would be Gillian Schutte's article reading South African women's poetry through Cixous's 'Medusa'.[140] Schutte analyses poems with a specific focus on feminine sexuality; however, the article does not posit any aspect of postcolonial theory in relation to South African women's poetry. The theory of feminine writing has not been applied to non-Western women's writing (specifically Turkish and Lebanese) alongside postcolonial theory. Therefore, I aim to fill this gap by employing a postcolonial feminine approach to Shafak and al-Shaykh's novels.

As demonstrated earlier in the Introduction, Shahrazad stands as a non-Western figure for the logic of feminine writing. Shahrazad has been analysed as a figure who explodes systems of power from within by many academics. Moore demonstrates Shahrazad's 'border-crossing' attributes, but she fails to recognise Shahrazad's position within contemporary non-Western women's literature.[141] Moore suggests that '[t]he Nights do not fundamentally challenge a heteronormative trajectory' because she considers the scope of Shahrazad's storytelling a uniform model, 'in which the female voice overwhelms the masculine fixing gaze, [which] does not adequately account for heterogeneous treatments of the vision/voice nexus in women's creative work'.[142] Although she notes forms of subversion such as (un)veiling in a postcolonial context, she fails to see how this form of subversion can carry forward the dynamics of the Nights. Moore does not acknowledge the concept of (un)veiling as a reiterative and performative act that is incarnated within Shahrazad's storytelling as a form of disguise as well as resistance.

Hanadi al-Samman's analysis of contemporary Arab women's writing is foundational in revisiting Shahrazad's narratives.[143] Al-Samman combines the

---

139 Lindsey Moore, *Arab, Muslim, Woman: Voice and Vision in Postcolonial Literature and Film* (Abingdon and New York: Routledge, 2008), p. 4.

140 Gillian Schutte, 'The Laugh of Medusa Heard in South African Women's Poetry', *Scrunity2*, 16, 2 (2011), pp. 42–55.

141 Moore, *Arab, Muslim, Woman*, p. 15.

142 Ibid., p. 15.

143 Hanadi al-Samman, *Anxiety of Erasure: Trauma, Authorship and the Diaspora in Arab Women's Writings* (Syracuse, NY: Syracuse UP, 2015).

figures of Shahrazad and 'the maw'udah' to demonstrate how cultural myths are revived in the context of contemporary political unrest by diaspora Arab women writers.[144] She argues that both Lebanese Civil War and diaspora experience give Arab women writers 'a unique opportunity to rewrite history' thus allowing them to interrogate gendered cultural discourses as well as political and personal traumas, whilst incorporating Shahrazad and the maw'udah into their narratives.[145] While the maw'udah is bodily 'erased' and silenced as she is buried, al-Samman suggests Shahrazad's voice is similarly erased in the epilogue when she abandons storytelling. Al-Samman therefore suggests that the recontextualization of both figures 'activate the corporal (al-maw'udah) and the literary (Shahrazad), thereby reuniting body and voice to heal the nation'.[146] Therefore, al-Samman argues for the potential of 'healing the nation' by embodying Shahrazad's voice within the image of 'the maw'udah', the buried infant girl 'for only a return to "roots" of [political and personal traumas] can deliver the resurrection of women's narration'.[147] Thus, this reunion both politicises and furthermore re-defines Shahrazad's role in contemporary diaspora women's writing. Along similar lines, I argue that al-Shaykh and Shafak transgress and re-define Shahrazad's position in a contemporary postcolonial context. While I suggest Shahrazad is perpetually re-contextualised in al-Shaykh and Shafak's works, I do not simply mean her voice. In contrast to al-Samman's analysis of Shahrazad as a literary voice, I would argue that Shahrazad in these narratives embodies the narrative whilst being embodied in her own narrative. Thus, both al-Shaykh and Shafak recognise Shahrazad's literary as well as corporeal existence in their novels.

Re-narratives of Shahrazad have also been analysed by Somaya Sami Sabry in a post 9/11 context with a particular notice of Orientalism. Sabry works on contemporary Arab-American women's literature and performances within the social and cultural sphere, from which they emerge. In this context, the re-narratives have mainly been viewed as responding to the appropriation of Arab-American women in a contemporary American literary context and the

---

144 'The maw'udah' means the buried infant girl in Arabic and refers to pre-Islamic practice of burying female infants by their fathers. The figure of the maw'udah is revisited as Syrian children resisted Assad's regime by writing on schools' walls, which al-Samman recognises as children impersonating Shahrazad. See al-Samman, pp. 1–2.

145 Ibid., p. 22.

146 Ibid., p. 3.

147 Ibid., p. 9.

appropriation of Shahrazad in an Orientalist context.[148] By contrast, I explore Shahrazad's storytelling in order to outline a new form of writing: postcolonial feminine writing. Therefore, Shahrazad's re-narratives do not merely respond to Orientalism, but they also challenge other power dynamics by re-writing the narrative, the gaze and the voice/silence.

Postcolonial Feminine Frames

Chapter I focuses on al-Shaykh's re-writing of *One Thousand and One Nights*. This novel is a re-narration of nineteen tales from the collection of the *Nights*. Al-Shaykh makes a specific decision to concentrate on the tales that contextualise gender norms and violence against women. While al-Shaykh is widely known for her earlier novels, especially *The Story of Zahra* and *Beirut Blues*, both of which contextualise the Lebanese Civil War (1975–1990), her re-telling of the *Nights* has been overlooked until the present day. There is a clear gap in the scholarly work available for this adaptation. I would suggest that this lack might be because this adaptation is different from her earlier novels in terms of setting and therefore does not provide an insight into the Lebanese national context. Al-Shaykh is mostly critiqued in terms of how she adapted war narratives in her novels and how she 'faithfully attempts to write of the world as she knows it'.[149] Therefore, I would suggest that al-Shaykh's novels have not been contextualised in literary theory nor considered in the context of feminine writing. While both *Zahra* and *Beirut Blues* focus on female characters who suffer as a result of the war and hence demonstrate trauma, these novels do not specifically offer narrative as the potential to a liberating space. Thus, I trace the instances of postcolonial feminine writing in al-Shaykh's *Nights* and focus on how the body and the text are re-written to be intricate and inseparable. I suggest that al-Shaykh makes a political intervention in the reception of non-Western women's writing by re-imagining social and gender norms as intersectional with the reclamation of Shahrazad's voice as a liberating figure. Indeed, I want to argue that this allows her to re-imagine new ways of existence such as marginalised characters and/or crossdressers in narration. I also argue how Shahrazad is a resistant figure and this notion of resistance is embedded within repeated cycle of storytelling.

Chapter II, which specifically focuses on Shafak's *The Gaze*, aims to move the context of Shahrazad's re-narration to a different form of power dynamics: the

---

148 Sabry, *Arab-American Women's Writing and Performance*, pp. 1–2.
149 Charles R. Larson, 'The Fiction of Hanan al-Shaykh, Reluctant Feminist', *World Literature Today*, 65, 1 (1991), pp. 14–7, p. 15.

gaze. This novel widely focuses on social norms and power dynamics in terms of how these dynamics dominate the gaze. Some critics focus on how the novel brings different traditions of narration together and reverses the dominant positions of the gaze, while other critics bring out the significance of symbolism or the interrogation of heteronormative characters in the novel. I argue that the novel creates liberating spaces for marginalised characters by mimicking Shahrazad's narrative style and content. Thus, I contextualise this novel with the concept of postcolonial feminine writing and aim to point out how the gaze is not simply reversed, but re-imagined for and by non-normative characters. The gaze is re-written as transforming, transformative and repetitive. I argue that this repetition of the gaze bears resemblance to (un)veiling in light of how both provide a disguise for the characters. In this chapter, I aim to interrogate how the gaze operates within power dynamics and whether it is possible to re-imagine these power dynamics through the lens of postcolonial feminine writing. I want to demonstrate how the novel allows for the undoing of various social and gender norms, welcoming the potential for a voice and gaze belonging to these marginalised characters. I discuss how the gaze becomes a narrative tool, through which marginalised bodies are continuously re-imagined.

The third and last literary chapter engages with Shafak's *Honour*. This chapter employs postcolonial feminine writing to the binary opposites of speech/silence and honour/shame, considering how these forms are restrictive for women and can be re-imagined. This novel also replicates Shahrazad's storytelling in terms of how the storyteller aims to narrate her mother's story to resist patriarchal power structures. Many critics contextualise this novel in terms of honour killings, especially in a Muslim context. However, it is widely overlooked that the novel specifically questions these social stereotypes around honour/shame by setting this honour killing in London, even though the perpetrator comes from a Muslim family. Another critic concentrates on the symbolism of the main character's name, Alexander, and considers this novel as part of Alexander narratives.[150] In contrast, I make observations regarding the position of Shahrazad's storytelling as constantly re-imagined through the figure of the storyteller. While the focus is predominantly on the context of honour and shame with regards to this novel, I want to show how these social norms are not always restrictive and opposing,

---

150 Alexander narratives/romances are 'epic and chivalric [narrative] traditions' focused on Alexander the Great. Petya Tsoneva Ivanova, *Negotiating Borderlines in Four Contemporary Migrant Writers from the Middle East* (Newcastle upon Tyne: Cambridge Scholars Publishing, 2018), p. 174.

but they have the potential to be liberating and complementing. I specifically interrogate how this novel deals with voice and silence by revealing that silence is not simply a submissive position for women. Rather, I want to argue the potential of different mediums of expressions through body in the case of women's silence. Indeed, I want to demonstrate how bodies themselves become languages in conveying resistance to patriarchal structures.

Conclusion makes a critical comparison of all chapters, presenting a final revision of how each chapter adopts and employs the concept of postcolonial feminine writing. That is, I specifically compare how each chapter analyses and re-imagines bodies as well as social and patriarchal power structures through the very figure of Shahrazad. While my first chapter aims to exemplify the technique of postcolonial feminine writing, my subsequent chapters introduce and analyse different notions (respectively, the gaze in Chapter II and shame and silence in Chapter III) within the framework of postcolonial feminine writing. This allows me to observe how Shahrazad is indeed mobile and transgressive of patriarchal narrative boundaries in a transnational context.

Chapter I: Re- writing the Storyteller: al- Shaykh's *One Thousand and One Nights* (2011)

Introduction

This chapter will specifically analyse Hanan al-Shaykh's *One Thousand and One Nights* as an example of postcolonial feminine writing in terms of how this text re-creates long-standing Shahrazadean tales for contemporary readers, with a distinct focus on misogyny or violence against women.[151] Here, I aim to locate postcolonial feminine writing within Shahrazad's narrative. I will interrogate how al-Shaykh re-imagines these tales as a way of re-forming social and gender norms and therefore imagines new ways of existing that do not conform to binary oppositions. Indeed, I argue that this chapter exemplifies how postcolonial feminine writing works with Shahrazad signifying the very figure of this concept. This chapter captures the very function of Shahrazad within the technique of re-imagining how we think and write social norms and hierarchies. This chapter demonstrates Shahrazad's function in the text as a character, a narrator and narrative technique for contemporary postcolonial writers. In doing so, this novel does not simply replicate the tales from *1001 Nights* but re-formulates these tales as the basis of transformation of these social and gender norms.

Al-Shaykh is a significant Lebanese author who has both represented Lebanese Civil War (1975–1990) and reflected upon her gendered experience of war in her novels.[152] However, I have chosen a novel that does not engage with war as I aim to analyse al-Shaykh's *Nights* and the figure of Shahrazad in a transnational

---

151 Hanan al-Shaykh, One Thousand and One Nights: A New Re-imagining (London: Bloomsbury, 2011, 2013). al-Shaykh has previously adapted these tales for Dash Arts' production, a play directed by Tim Supple, and then compiled them as a novel.

152 For detailed analyses of Lebanese War in literature see: Miriam Cooke, *War's Other Voices: Women Writers on the Lebanese Civil War* (Cambridge: Cambridge UP, 1988); Evelyn Accad, *Sexuality and War: Literary Masks of the Middle East* (New York and London: New York University Press, 1990); Lamia Rustum Shehadeh, 'The War in Lebanon', in *Women and War in Lebanon*, ed. by Lamia Rustum Shehadeh (Gainesville, FL: University Press of Florida, 1999).

context. Here, I do not want to reduce al-Shaykh's writing to the Lebanese context precisely because her novels exceed this context even if they emerge from there. As this chapter itself works to exemplify postcolonial feminine writing, I will strictly focus on Shahrazad's narrative and this novel by al-Shaykh. This novel offers a significant position for postcolonial feminine writing specifically because al-Shaykh allows Shahrazad to develop her own voice and to intervene in the reproduction of social norms in a contemporary literary sense. Therefore, this chapter focuses on how the text returns to and reiterates the voice of a long-standing female storyteller as a political and literary response to patriarchal norms. I would suggest that understanding how this novel is written would be central to understanding the concept of postcolonial feminine writing. For this reason, I will specifically focus on how this interrogation of bodies creates a process of (un)veiling insofar as diverse bodies are re-produced by means of subversive repetition.

Here, I offer the concept of postcolonial feminine writing as a repetitive process through which social norms can be re-imagined. While this concept does not guarantee that these norms can be re-formulated as completely new forms, it opens up the potential for a liberating space to re-think and re-write them. I would argue that the text re-creates bodies as hybrid and plural, and thus marginalised, and thereby presents the potential to explore diversity and multiplicity by repeating similar stories with different characters and in differing genres. In particular, I will note the ways in which this novel challenges the notion of corporeal bodies as heteronormative and definitive. The narrators and characters use different forms of disguise that I name as (un)veiling in my Introduction. The novel specifically engages with the perception of manipulation and expresses how it becomes a significant means of resistance for the oppressed characters. This is an imperative position within postcolonial feminine writing in terms of how these tales are narrated by multiple narrators to give voice to silenced and oppressed subjects.

The novel adopts the same narrative structure as the *Nights* and similarly, Shahrazad's initial appearance in the text is as a character and a passive participant. Thereafter, Shahrazad the character evolves into Shahrazad the narrator, not only actively participating within these tales, but also reciting them and controlling the tone and message of the tales. Suzanne Gauch points out that '[b]ecause the tale lacks an author, the only master-or rather mistress-presiding over these changes and challenges is Shahrazad herself. [...] Translators and other adaptors [...] slipped into Shahrazad's role as they reshaped' the flow of

the tales to invoke curiosity in their target audiences.[153] Thus, as an adaptor and
re-creator of Shahrazad's tales, the author al-Shaykh is identified with Shahrazad
the narrator by determining the flow and steering the purpose of the novel as
resistance to gendered violence. The author explains her selection of tales in an
interview as intentionally 'dark, complex, [and] violent, [and] about misogynists,
men who either killed their wives or their lovers', compatible with the frame
tale of Shahrayar the King, who kills his wife (upon catching her in the act of
adultery) and his subsequent wives (because of his vengeance against women)
.[154] Therefore, the subsequent tales assume the position of a spiritual guide to
transform the perspective of the audience, namely Shahrayar and the readers,
on women by demonstrating how oppression makes women more manipulative
and resistant. While this position appears to restrict women, it is never stable and
thus always open to the manipulation of 'porous [and] fragile' borders.[155]

The novel consists of nineteen inter-connected tales. Each tale is written in a
different genre ranging from satire, comedy, tragedy, detective fiction and magic
realism to poetry. In the early tales, Shahrazad addresses the King directly while
the following tales disguise her voice. She initially addresses him 'o happy and
wise king' in the early tales and I would suggest that it is Shahrazad's intention to
appear as if she conforms to the restrictions sanctioned by the king. Shahrazad
seemingly submits to him when she addresses him and waits for his verdict on
her storytelling every dawn until she knows that he is addicted and attentive to
her stories. She is granted access to the role of storyteller, who is listened to by
the King and yet the address used in the previous tales is lost as an indication of
Shahrazad's agency as a storyteller. The tales are narrated as interwoven, with distinct narrators (man, woman and queer) while the reader and the audience must
adapt to the change in tone and the gender and sexuality of the narrator. This
shift in power dynamics as a result of unreliable gender and social hierarchies is
significant because it demonstrates that the boundaries between structures are
negotiable and can result in the subversion of power dynamics.

Shahrazad and other characters resist and manipulate the patriarchal narrative discourse. Rather than simply focusing on how this re-narrative differs

153 Suzanne Gauch, *Liberating Shahrazad: Feminism, Postcolonialism and Islam*
(Minneapolis, MN: The University of Minnesota Press, 2007), pp. 2–36.
154 Mcardle, Molly, 'Author Q&A: Hanan al-Shaykh's New Shahrazad', L J Reviews 26th
April 2013, < http://www.libraryjournal.com/?detailStory=author-qa-hanan-al-shay
khs-new-shahrazad > [accessed 2nd October 2021].
155 Fatema Mernissi, *Scheherazade Goes West* (New York: Washington Square Press,
2001), p. 46.

from other narratives of *Nights*, I want to argue that this novel is an important re-telling by clearly showing how postcolonial feminine writing gives the appearance of conformity insofar as the patriarchal authority still appears to be in charge of Shahrazad's life. This also creates a space for Shahrazad to undo these patriarchal boundaries from within. The very content of the novel mirrors the form and narrative techniques. Not only is the content perpetually repeated in different contexts by different narrators, it also follows the structure of postponing the end and keeping suspense for the audience. All the while Shahrazad is narrating others' tales, she is re-narrating her own story and re-inventing her own position within the narrative.

The frame tale begins by questioning the rigidity of the social roles. The wife, whom Shahrayar viciously murders, has authority over her slaves that is based upon a shift of power. This nameless queen orders a black slave to have an intercourse with her. However, her authority is questionable since the slave addresses her as 'slut' in a demeaning way. The tales Shahrazad narrates begin with three independent young women and their superiority over their male guests. The male guests are accepted into the three women's house on condition that they 'speak not of what concerns you, lest you hear what does not please'.[156] After the male guests witness the women flog two dogs as they weep, they question the women's motives: '[t]he gentlemen wish to know why you beat the two bitches until you had no strength left and yet then wept for them, kissed them, wiped away their tears' even though they vow not to inquire before they are admitted into the house.[157] To this exchange, the women's aid responds by questioning '[s]hall we behead them this instant?'.[158] The novel subverts the situation of Shahrazad and Shahrayar as the guests encounter a death threat upon their inquiries and are expected to share their life stories. It follows the same intention of Shahrazad: evading the death threat by pleasing the oppressor, but in this case with three women (named The Mistress of the House, The Doorkeeper, and the Shopper) in authority.

After the guests' narration begin, one of the male guests is revealed to be Haroun al-Rashid, the caliph, and that brings forth a temporary fluctuation of power. I would suggest that all roles are transforming in the novel and therefore not heteronormative or conforming. The novel takes a new direction when the caliph decrees that the young women should be wedded, and thus the three

---

156 Al-Shaykh, *Nights*, p. 36.
157 Ibid., pp. 40–1.
158 Ibid., p. 41.

women begin narrating new tales to delay their doom. With these multiple narrators, Shahrazad successfully disguises herself and narrates her own tale with Shahrayar from a distanced perspective. The last tale in the novel is that of Shahrazad and Shahrayar's which ends with an ellipsis creating a sense of never-ending continuation. She tells stories of different human beings: young, old, man, woman, queer, wily, manipulative, innocent, plotting or trapped. Presenting humans with different traits, Shahrazad aims to prove to Shahrayar that manipulation and resistance are second nature to the oppressed and that authority is not always a reliable perspective. The use of multiple narrative voices serves to resist being restrained to a one-dimensional perspective and thus displaces a single authority. I would therefore suggest that multiple narrators reveal that there are always multiple perspectives in a tale and therefore one voice is unreliable while they also enable more women access to narrative voice, which was previously reserved for men.[159]

Shahrazad's difference from the king's previous female companions is that she becomes the 'mistress' of the word. Shahrazad chooses to marry Shahrayar herself against her father's warnings that she risks being murdered. She threatens her father saying that she will complain about his reluctance to present her to the king. As she unsettles her paternal authority, the novel shows that Shahrazad has the potential to resist patriarchal authority. With the knowledge of the fates of Shahrayar's previous brides, she does not set out to be only a one-night sexual companion to Shahrayar. She enlists her sister to help her gain access to her voice and storytelling. Her sister shall ask for a story and Shahrazad begins her tale, in turn engaging the king in her narration to survive each night, ceasing his actions, 'thereby saving both [her] own life and those of all the girls who remain in the kingdom.'[160] I would suggest that Shahrazad's engagement with her sister is a form of postcolonial feminine writing because it demonstrates how a woman enables (can enable) the other woman to speak. Shahrazad's survival each night (and the survival of subsequent wives if she failed) depends on allowing women to discover and explore the immense resources of their own bodies and voices.

The novel has an open ending, which begins to repeat Shahrazad's own story. Al-Shaykh concludes the novel with 'until one day...' leaving her readers in

---

159 Consistent with the story-within-story narrative structure, the text enables different characters to be storytellers in subsequent tales, such as 'The Mistress of the House's Tale', 'The Doorkeeper's Tale' and 'The Shopper's Tale' in which these women offer their own perspectives to challenge the stories previously told by men.

160 Al-Shaykh, *Nights*, p. 10.

suspense. This is a deliberate position to assume because Shahrazad's storytelling cannot be contained by the boundaries of an epilogue as was the case in the European versions of the *Nights*. This last tale is narrated from the perspective of another female character, which shows how the novel creates a space in the narration for a strong, intelligent and liberating storyteller by allowing 'other tongues to speak'. I would suggest that that Shahrazad's tales have a therapeutic effect on the king and tames his 'violent, murderous soul'.[161] As I explored in my Introduction, postcolonial feminine writing demonstrates the potential of an infinite ending. As there are different options with which to conclude the *Nights* by different re-creators, an epilogue would be misleading. Therefore, the novel allows for different narrators to maintain the narrative, and this repetition of narration proves to be a source of language that women can get inside of and thereby re-imagine restrictive social and gender boundaries.

The *Nights* has been largely overlooked by critics. I would suggest that this is because it is a re-telling unlike al-Shaykh's previous novels, which specifically focus on Lebanese characters and settings. The only exception to this would be Nazry Bahrawi's article focusing on the re-writing tradition of the *Nights* as a technique of translation studies.[162] The article makes relevant comparisons between al-Shaykh's compilation and earlier adaptations of the *Nights*. Bahrawi suggests that the significance of this adaptation lies in al-Shaykh being the only Arab woman writer to re-narrate the tales and that 'Al-Shaykh makes up for lost opportunities by inscribing into it the theme of power and its subversions, making hers possibly the cultural rewrite most congruent to the modernist ethics of human rights'.[163] Here, Bahrawi highlights the significance of al-Shaykh as a female author because al-Shaykh captures the very essence of Shahrazad as a liberating and potentially feminist narrator. Although Bahrawi alludes to the form of the novel as 'feminine', he fails to contextualise it as a form of feminine writing. My own criticism clarifies the ways this novel is an example of postcolonial feminine writing whilst repeating similar tales to the previous adaptations. I would suggest that this novel fundamentally differs from its predecessors specifically because it recognises Shahrazad as the most prominent narrator and further allows her to intervene in the patriarchal literary discourse through subversive storytelling.

---

161 Al-Shaykh, *Nights*, p. 288.
162 Nazry Bahrawi, 'A Thousand and One Rewrites: Translating Modernity in the *Arabian Nights*', *Journal of World Literature*, 1, 3 (2016), pp. 357–70.
163 Ibid., p. 365.

Furthermore, I use a selection of other secondary sources on al-Shaykh in order to articulate the difference of my own criticism of *the Nights* from what has been written on her other works. Her two earlier novels, *The Story of Zahra* and *Beirut Blues*, both of which narrate the influence of Lebanese Civil War on their heroines, have been of controversial interest to Arabophone critics.[164] Samira Aghacy points out that the war changes the exclusivity of the public space which belonged to men and sex workers and now also belongs to 'respectable women like Zahra'.[165] By having sex with a sniper of the civil war, 'Zahra transgresses all spatial boundaries [...] to empower and free herself'.[166] Thus, for Aghacy, the protagonist is empowered socially and sexually by 'the war city'.[167] Marianne Marroum also works on *The Story of Zahra* with a different standpoint. She explains that the novel is not exclusively focused on Zahra, because there are two other narrators, her uncle and her husband of a short period, who are both expatriates in Africa. They see Zahra as a way 'to make a triumphant comeback in physical absentia to [their] homeland'.[168] Marroum points to the fact that the novel is written during the war and it is influenced by the social problem that occurs as a result of the war.

On the one hand, Charles R. Larson criticises how al-Shaykh's protagonists are 'more acted upon than active: the victims of an Islamic patriarchy'.[169] Larson finds Zahra indecisive and directionless, and belittles al-Shaykh's work as 'faithfully attempting to write of the world as she knows it'.[170] Larson obviously disregards that al-Shaykh uses Shahrazadean techniques to represent the social problems that she witnessed, and that she does not entrap her protagonists in an 'Islamic patriarchy'. Larson's article also provides an unveiled photo of al-Shaykh,

164 *The Story of Zahra* is a coming-of-age novel about Zahra, her earlier life, marriage, sexual adventures and the freedom that war brings her. *Beirut Blues* is an epistolary novel narrated by its heroine, Asmahan, who writes letters to the living, dead or objects, and these letters narrate her life before and after the war.
165 Samira Aghacy, 'Contemporary Lebanese Fiction: Modernization without Modernity', *International Journal of Middle East Studies*, 38, 4 (2006), pp. 561–80, p. 567.
166 Ibid., p. 567.
167 Samira Aghacy, 'Lebanese Women's Fiction: Urban Identity and the Tyranny of the Past', *International Journal of Middle East Studies*, 33, 4 (2001), pp. 503–23, p. 508.
168 Marianne Marroum, 'What's So Great About Home?: Roots, Nostalgia, and Return in Andree Chedid's *La Maison sans racines* and Hanan al-Shaykh's *Hikayat Zahra*', *Comparative Literature Studies*, 45, 4 (2008), pp. 491–513, p. 509.
169 Charles R. Larson, 'The Fiction of Hanan al-Shaykh, Reluctant Feminist', *World Literature Today*, 65, 1 (1991), pp. 14–7, p. 14.
170 Ibid., p. 15.

which problematizes the author's position within so-called Islamic patriarchy. On the other hand, Walid El Hamamsy highlights how Asmahan is confessional in a 'process of liberation and self-discovery' in *Beirut Blues*.[171] Through her letters, El Hamamsy claims that '[Asmahan] can enjoy human relations which have been denied to her by her environment'.[172] El Hamamsy connects Asmahan's letter-writing to Shahrazad's storytelling that frees her '[when] she is given a voice with which to express herself and to be heard'.[173] Thus, Asmahan's autobiographical writing works as a means of self-liberation. These critics largely neglect al-Shaykh's subversive storytelling even when they recognise the protagonists' search for self-liberation. Conversely, I want to contextualise al-Shaykh's *Nights* as one of the pioneers, which re-narrates Shahrazad's tales to create liberating spaces within narrative and offer the potential to transform social norms and hierarchies by constantly re-imagining them. Therefore, I suggest that al-Shaykh enables Shahrazad's and other marginalised people's voices to be heard and listened to by the audience/readers. In doing so, the *Nights* exemplifies postcolonial feminine writing in how the text re-imagines social and gender hierarchies through the very way in which the tales are narrated and how voice emerges.

Whilst my discussion of Cixous and feminine writing is more focused on rethinking embodiment discursively, I want to acknowledge the embodied potentials of Shahrazad's narrative with a focus on how new materialist feminism offers another dimension to rethinking the very material existence of women's bodies. New materialist feminists such as Stacy Alaimo propose integrating human corporeality into feminist studies.[174] Stacy Alaimo and Susan Hekman bring together various strands of bodily engagement with nature and re-contextualise the materiality of human bodies in *Material Feminisms*. Building on feminist science critics such as Donna Haraway and Karen Barad, Alaimo and Hekman address 'the dis-ease in contemporary feminist theory and practice that resulted from the loss of the material' and seek to move beyond a discursive

---

171 Walid El Hamamsy, 'Epistolary Memory: Revisiting Traumas in Women's Writing', *Alif: Journal of Comparative Poetics*, 30 (2010), pp. 150–75, p. 165.

172 Ibid., p. 166.

173 Ibid., p. 170.

174 Stacy Alaimo's other works such as *Undomesticated Ground* (2000), *Bodily Natures* (2010) and *Exposed* (2016) also offer insight into her conception of trans-corporeality. Here, I will focus on the introduction of and Alaimo's essay in *Material Feminisms* mainly because they propose a fundamental understanding of 'trans-corporeality' grounded in contemporary materialist feminist theories.

engagement with the material.[175] Moreover, they aim to deconstruct the material/discursive dichotomy and thus interrogate how the human interacts with the nature of 'more-than-human'. This deconstruction is a significant 'turn' in feminist studies specifically because it allows for a discussion about 'the materiality of the body as itself an active, sometimes recalcitrant, force'.[176] While Alaimo and Hekman disrupt the binary oppositions of human/nature, they also propose the mechanism to engage with and comprehend the body both materially and discursively through their reformulation of materialist feminism. Thus, the materialist turn in feminist studies would also help us understand the significance of re-uniting women with their bodies in the discourse of feminine writing as Alaimo and Hekman assert '[w]omen *have* bodies [that] have pain as well as pleasure [and] are subject to medical interventions'.[177] This demonstrates how women's bodies are susceptible to external interventions and therefore forever transforming through various means such as medical and or environmental interventions such as illnesses and 'breakages'.[178]

More importantly, Alaimo re-imagines 'human corporeality as trans-corporeality, in which the human opens out into a more-than-human world, underlines the extent to which the corporeal substance of the human is ultimately inseparable from "the environment"'.[179] Therefore, trans-corporeality grounds the human subject within and through nature by exposing their biological, social and 'natural' entanglements. By visualising a 'contact zone' between human and nature, Alaimo shows how not only human and nature are inseparable, but also neither are fixed in their materiality. Alaimo argues that feminist theories particularly refrain from engaging with the corporeal body as they assume that nature is 'fixed' in its materiality.[180] By engaging with the matter of the body through trans-corporeality, Alaimo offers a new way to 'render biological determinism "nonsense"'.[181] Several examples such as intersex cells in the human body or

175 Stacy Alaimo, and Susan Hekman, *Material Feminisms* (Bloomington, IN: Indiana UP, 2008), p. 6.
176 Ibid., p. 4.
177 Ibid., p. 4, emphasis in original.
178 Sara Ahmed engages with several forms of 'breakages' in *Living a Feminist Life* as I discuss on pp. 49–50.
179 Alaimo and Hekman, *Material Feminisms*, p. 14.
180 Stacy Alaimo, 'Trans-corporeal Feminisms and the Ethical Space of Nature', in *Material Feminisms*, ed. by Stacy Alaimo, and Susan Hekman (Bloomington, IN: Indiana UP, 2008), p. 241.
181 Ibid., p. 241.

some species of fungi with 'more than 28,000 sexes', as demonstrated by Myra J. Hird in 'Naturally Queer', render the binary form of hetero-sexism 'unnatural' and non-heteronormative.[182] Building on Hird, Alaimo argues that this queer biology 'contests [...] normative hetero-biology [and] its claim to objectivity and neutrality'.[183] Therefore, trans-corporeality challenges the very grounds of essentialism in how it blurs the boundary between human and queer nature/biology. To turn to Cixous, I want to argue that Cixous is not simply essentialist due to her, albeit pre-dominantly discursive, engagement with the body. Cixous reveals how the binary oppositions such as culture/nature are restrictive and offers ways to move beyond these restrictions in language whereas it is the materiality of the body in materialist feminisms. Furthermore, Cixous attests to the significance of matter when she utters 'anything having to do with the body should be explored, from the functional to the libidinal, to the imaginary [and] femininity derives from the body, from the anatomical [and] the biological difference'.[184] As femininity is explored as biological difference(s), and not simply defined within the biological opposition, it provides a potential path to return to the material body as well. While Cixous may still be considered essentialist for her close engagement with women's bodies in terms of the anatomical, she refrains from enforcing a hetero-sexist feminine ideal on women. Rather, I suggest that Cixous offers new and imaginative ways to engage with the body (such as blurring the boundary between monster and human through the figure/head of Medusa), similar to what Alaimo argues. Therefore, Cixous's 'Medusa' becomes one of the texts that inform my analysis of non-Western women's texts as postcolonial feminine writing.

Sara Ahmed also offers an imaginative way to engage with the materiality of the body through the figure of feminist killjoy in *Living a Feminist Life*. Ahmed considers how the figure of the feminist killjoy 'is doing more than saying the wrong thing: she is getting in the way of something, the achievement or accomplishment of the family or some *we* or another, which is created by what is not said' when she speaks.[185] When the feminist killjoy appears, Ahmed insists, she interrupts dominant conversations/narratives by exposing individual, familial or institutional problems. Through the figure of killjoy, Ahmed is able

---

182 Myra J. Hird, 'Naturally Queer', *Feminist Theory*, 5, 1 (2004), pp. 85–9, p. 86.

183 Alaimo, 'Trans-corporeal Feminisms', p. 241.

184 Hélène Cixous, and Susan Sellers, *White Ink: Interviews on Sex, Text and Politics* (Stocksfield: Acumen, 2008), p. 66.

185 Sara Ahmed, *Living a Feminist Life* (London and Durham, NC: Duke UP, 2017), p. 37.

to consequently return to and reflect on her own experiences of being a killjoy for her family, friends or colleague and employers. This connection between the killjoy and Ahmed herself gives her the opportunity to explore and re-write her body as material and metaphorical.[186] The image of the feminist killjoy is explored as a fragile entity as when she encounters 'brick walls' in her wilful feminism she might easily 'shatter'. This feeling of shattering, breaking of the body, is familiar to feminist killjoys as '[i]t might be that in order to inhabit certain spaces we have to block recognition of just how wearing they are: when the feeling catches us, it might be at the point when it is just too much. You are shattered'.[187] So, coming up against the same brick walls, be it racist or sexist remarks in workplace or some external space, will break or shutter the body of the killjoy in a literary space. It is a metaphorical breakage of the will or morale of the feminist killjoy. Moreover, Ahmed uses this breakage as the main point to explore the corporeality of her own body because '[w]e learn: how what matters, matters' when something breaks.[188] By drawing on the fragility of the killjoy body, Ahmed points out the different experiences of corporeal diversity of bodies: '[a] body can be broken. If we keep coming up against walls, it feels like we can shatter into a million pieces. Tiny little pieces. **Bodies break. That too. Though that is not all that bodies do**'.[189] Here, 'that too' refers Ahmed's own temporary experience of disability which helps her re-construct orientation towards the phenomenon of breaking because '[i]n a shattering story there is often a *too*, a *too* that often falls on what falls'.[190] So her body breaks *too* when she literally falls on a hard space even if 'that is not all that bodies do'.

Whilst the metaphorical breakage of the killjoy leads to 'a tear in the social fabric', as the killjoy breaks the chain of injustice in return, the corporeal breakage of her body (a fracture in her pelvis) results in a different bodily experience.[191]

---

186 Ahmed gives insightful discussion of wilfulness and how wilful subjects become wilful objects in their act of wilfulness in *Wilful Subjects* (2014). Ahmed constructs a link between wilfulness and embodiment through the concept of the 'free will' and the will of objects. I choose to engage with *Living a Feminist Life* because Ahmed's discussion of material and metaphorical body through the image and body of the killjoy supports my argument around embodiment and literature. See Sara Ahmed, *Wilful Subjects* (London and Durham, NC: Duke UP, 2014).
187 Ibid., p. 164.
188 Ibid., p. 165.
189 Ibid., p. 180, bold in original.
190 Ibid., p. 164.
191 Ibid., p. 171.

Through her short-term disability, Ahmed discusses how she experiences life differently since 'disability is worldly [because of] the different ways you are treated,
the opening of doors, concerned faces, the closing of doors, rigid indifference,
[…] the little bumps on the street [that] became walls that took a huge amount
of energy just to get over or to get around'.[192] I would therefore suggest the temporary experience of disability opens up the possibility of embodying different
bodies and different corporeal experiences that experience 'little bumps on the
street' as brick walls that are difficult to overcome. Thus, the point of breaking
also becomes the point of uniting for Ahmed with the killjoy figure. Because
a break changes a person's experience of what-is-more-than-him/her, even in
its healing, it alters the material body and 'you are no longer as you were'.[193]
Reflecting on Eli Clare's experience of cerebral palsy, Ahmed discusses how dis-
abled bodies encounter 'brick walls' when the world is organised 'into straight
lines [and] narrow spaces'.[194] Ahmed argues that '[f]rom a shattering, a story
can be told, one that finds in fragility the source of a connection. […] A break
can offer another claim to being, being in question as a break in being, recog-
nizing breaking as making a difference in the present, shaping the present'.[195]
While the break previously allowed the space for Ahmed to transition from the
metaphorical to the corporeal, it once again becomes the point for her to transition into the metaphorical. Ahmed allows the fracture an embodied experience
through the killjoy figure, who then allows Ahmed an embodied experience of
breakage through her temporary disability. In doing so, Ahmed's engagement
with the materiality of bodies supports Alaimo's theoretical engagement with
trans-corporeality. Alaimo's suggestion that bodies are forever transforming is
reflected here as the mobility of the body as material/discursive. However, it also
unsettles trans-corporeality as Alaimo predominantly engages with the material despite her claim to disrupt the material/discursive dichotomy. I would
argue that Ahmed indeed tears down this dichotomy by blurring the boundaries
between the material and the metaphorical. Uniting her corporeal body with
the figurative killjoy body, I suggest that Ahmed makes it possible for stories to
offer a comprehensive understanding of diverse bodily experiences as well as
engage with material and discursive bodies simultaneously. Even though stories

192 Ibid., pp. 180–1.
193 Ibid., p. 182.
194 Ibid., p. 182, Ahmed's reference is to Eli Clare, *Exile and Pride: Disability, Querness, and Liberation* (Durham, NC: Duke UP, 1999, repr. 2015).
195 Ahmed, *Living a Feminist Life*, p. 183.

do not alter the materiality of these bodies, they allow for these diverse bodies to be recognised, thus offering 'another claim to being' and 'shaping the present'. Although *Postcolonial Feminine Writing* do not reflect specifically on the corporeality of bodies, it works on the significance of recognising the diversity of bodies in narratives. I argue that literature helps us to develop theoretical thinking on societal and bodily norms. Thus, Ahmed's theoretical and very poetical engagement with bodies would support my argument how bodies can be repeatedly re-imagined as diverse in non-Western women's writing. As such, Shahrazad's re-narratives enable us to re-imagine bodies as both corporeal and narratorial, and thus I analyse how Shahrazad inhabits her own narrative on diverse levels in the following sections.

Repetition of Desires: Shahrazad Re-creating Social and Gender Hierarchies

Shahrazad exists within the novel on multiple levels as a character, narrator and the creator of the narrative technique of postcolonial feminine writing. I therefore argue that the text's enactment of postcolonial feminine writing predates Shahrazad's initiation as a character. The novel is opened by a third person narrator, who introduces the story of King Shahrayar, his brother Shahzaman, and facilitates Shahrazad's entrance into the tale primarily as a character and subsequently as a narrator. I would suggest that her initiation into the tale is particularly significant because the text becomes the epitome of postcolonial feminine writing by enabling Shahrazad to gain access to the patriarchal narrative discourse and reclaim her voice by re-forming this discourse from within. Shahrazad constructs a repetitive cycle of storytelling and thereby manipulates the king's narrative desire and his sexual desire as she has intercourse with him every night before resuming her tales. Shahrazad uses this sexual desire to her advantage as it becomes the means through which she intervenes in various power structures and acts of violence. Similarly, al-Shaykh's novel begins with a disruption of patriarchal power structures with sexuality. I suggest that the novel constructs the practice of sexual desire as having the potential to disrupt power structures from within these social and gender hierarchies as well as to re-imagine alternatives for them.

The *Nights* begins this disruption early as an intervention in power structures when Shahzaman's queen has intercourse with her slave.[196] The queen's

---

196 Al-Shaykh, *Nights*, p. 4.

performance of sexual desire undermines the patriarchal authority over her body. Shahzaman discovers his wife 'lying in the arms of one of the kitchen boys' and exclaims that 'my wife has betrayed me, but with whom? With another king? A general in the army? No – with a kitchen boy!'.[197] Shahzaman is affected most, not through his experience of being betrayed, but because he is cheated on with someone of a lower-class status. This is a significant act in the tale because it complicates both class and sexuality norms. On the one hand, the queen undermines the king's authority over her body even temporarily. Furthermore, this also calls his authority over his slaves into question as the kitchen boy disregards Shahzaman's royal status. On the other hand, the queen abuses her power by initiating a relationship with the slave because the slave is forced into a compromising position with the king. However, it marks the point whereby sexual desire may indeed be acknowledged as the basis of an intervention in social class structures. When Shahzaman was unaware of her infidelity, she appeared to conform to his rules. Nevertheless, she reclaims the power over her own body. The very idea of this woman's resistance is conveyed on and through her body. By having sex with a person, who is considered altogether unsuitable for a queen, she invents a form of resistance making her sexual existence possible within the patriarchal systems of power.

The novel repeatedly interrogates the reliability of gender and sexuality norms. Shahzaman realises that his brother is also suffering from a similar fate. Shahrayar's wife cheats on Shahrayar with a number of slaves. Shahzaman witnesses the queen enter the courtyard alongside ten white slaves and ten black slaves, who are dressed as women and later revealed to be men. The slaves make pairs, the queen invites Mas'ud the slave, and they all have intercourse in Shahrayar's garden. Afterwards, they re-dress and depart from the courtyard all dressed as women. The text suggests that this sexual spree is repeated as soon as Shahrayar departs from the palace. Here, the slaves may interrupt social and gender norms on multiple levels as evidenced by Shahzaman's reaction. While his own doom left him miserable, seeing his brother being cheated by not only his wife 'but all [his] concubines and slaves too' gives him ease because he understands '[this is a] treacherous world, which fails to distinguish between a sovereign king and a nobody'.[198] It is the beginning of the recognition of the unreliability of social class. Because Shahrayar's authority is not only threatened by his wife, but his concubines and male slaves, his position is not a rigid and

---

197 Ibid., p. 2.
198 Al-Shaykh, *Nights*, p. 4.

invincible authority. Here, the text suggests that the patriarchal authority is perpetually unsettled by people who, they are under the impression, are of a lower status than themselves. This indeed introduces how the concept of (un)veiling works and presents Shahrazad's initiation into the storytelling. It is particularly the repetitiveness of the queen's and other slaves' performance of sexual desire which makes this disguise relevant and successful. By undressing as men and re-dressing as women they follow a pattern of (un)veiling. As the slaves perpetually (un)veil, they show how gender norms can be complex and deceptive. Here, while black slaves seem simply unthreatening and ostensibly conform to the king's authority, they can overlook these power structures when they are disrobed. I would therefore suggest that the text traces the potential of agency to repetition. Although it might be a temporary shift of power, when Shahrayar is already elsewhere, it still demonstrates the possibility of liberation for both the queen and her slaves. The fact that Shahrazad recognises the significance of repetition and uses it to prolong her narrative distinguishes her from the queen. Shahrazad's intervention is long-lasting particularly as she connects sexual desire to narrative desire.

I want to take a closer look at the queen and Mas'ud's relationship because it effectively shows how systems of power are perpetually re-defined. The queen clearly exerts the power of her status when she is involved with a slave. She objectifies her slave and abuses him for her desire. However, it is not long before her authority over Mas'ud is undermined. Mas'ud, who jumps from the tree to the ground, likened to an animal in his act, addresses the queen '[w]hat do you want, you slut? Allow me to present Sa'ad al-Din Mas'ud', pointing at his penis.[199] This suggests that the performance of sexuality between the queen and her subject is more intricate. Her authority is immediately challenged when Mas'ud uses 'slut' as a derogatory term to address the queen and identifies his penis as a pleasure-provider and a person of its own significance. I suggest that the queen's authority is repeatedly shifting depending on her performance of sexual desire. While it allows her to adopt a temporary position of power over Shahrayar, it is almost always unstable. However, the potential of Mas'ud's authority over both Shahrayar and the queen is particularly important. The text demonstrates that he does not remain constricted to his so-called inferiority. Quite the opposite, Mas'ud the slave legitimises his existence by reclaiming his own power through this transaction. He challenges both her and Shahrayar's authority by conducting relations with his wife. Mas'ud single-handedly controls the queen's

---

199 Al-Shaykh, *Nights*, p. 7.

sexual desire. Moreover, I would suggest that he uses it to his own advantage because he is able to re-define his social and sexual boundaries from within power structures that already assumes his so-called inferiority. This suggests that the potential of disrupting hierarchies does not merely belong to women but also other marginalised characters. By re-formulating his position as a sex slave to a dominant partner, Mas'ud 'seizes' the occasion to have power and speak back to so-called class superiority (as in calling the queen a 'slut').

The act of repetition is not simply a formal quality as the content is similarly repeated. This repetition demonstrates that defining a feminine practice of resistance is not possible by other characters in the novel. The text repeats the queen and Mas'ud's tale by placing Shahrayar and Shahzaman in Mas'ud's position. The royal brothers encounter a woman, who has been kidnapped and hidden in a locked chest by a demon. When the demon goes to sleep, the woman seizes the opportunity to resist the demon's control and reclaim her power over her body. The woman sees the brothers from under the tree and forces them to have intercourse with her by using a death threat. They fall from the tree just as Mas'ud does and copulate with the demon's wife. I suggest that the text re-defines their social and gendered positions as they become this woman's sexual objects. Fedwa Malti-Douglas points out that 'sexual roles are reversed but so are social ones. [I]f the black slave descending from the tree can be thought of as an ape, so too now can be the royal brothers'.[200] This suggests that a repeated cycle of tales reproduces similar systems of power in shifting contexts. The text indicates the possibility of a temporary reclamation of power as '[e]ach time she climaxed [she] looked at the sleeping demon, as if determined to spite him, and take revenge'.[201] The demon's wife then seizes their rings and shows them the ninety-eight rings in her purse, all of which represent the men she previously slept with. The woman defends her position because '[h]e keeps me trapped beneath the raging sea, believing he can possess me, and keep me apart and unseen from all others. But he is a fool, for he does not know that no one can prevent a woman from fulfilling her desires, even if she is hidden under the roaring sea, jealously guarded by a demon'.[202] Here, I want to suggest that the narrative of the novel is indeed experimental with its representation of sexual desire like Shahrazad's storytelling. By experimenting with different systems of power in various tales, the text suggests the very experimentality of liberation. While the brothers were

---

200 Malti-Douglas, Woman's Body, Woman's Word, p. 18.
201 Al-Shaykh, Nights, p. 217.
202 Ibid., p. 217.

rulers and liberated in the previous tale, the demon's wife challenges their social and gendered positions. I would therefore suggest that the text does not inherently guarantee liberation as a result. Thus, the tales are repeated formally and content-wise to constantly re-define these social structures even if it is a risk to the self. This is a very deliberate Shahrazadean narrative technique as she takes a risk with every new tale. She resumes her tales each night for an indefinite period of time precisely because she is experimenting with her liberation by continuing her narrative. Likewise, the demon's wife keeps her sexual relations with multiple men. In doing so, she takes big risks as if she grows a set of wings to fly away from her boundaries. This exemplifies the very mission of postcolonial feminine writing by 'finding hidden crossovers' and re-claiming her desires even when she is supposed to be restrained.

The demon's wife is resistant to her restraints even though this is not acknowledged by the demon. The fact that her resistance is not recognised by her captor does not mean she does not successfully resist. It is also important to note that Shahrayar's interpretation of this incident, which results in him setting out on a murderous rampage targeting women because he indeed recognises her reclamation of power over her body and manipulation of him. Shahrayar tells his brother that they are lucky to witness that '[t]his demon believes he has the woman imprisoned in a glass chest, [...] kept beneath the sea [...], and yet she has slept with one hundred men. Now we can go home to our kingdoms, but let us be without women. You will see what I shall do'.[203] Shahrayar understands the kidnapped woman is the demon's captive under the sea and considers her reaction as proof that all women are manipulative and dishonest even when they are imprisoned. The novel presents this scene to illustrate that both his late wife and the demon's captive resist being imprisoned by using their sexuality. The patriarchal authority, represented by the royal brothers, fails to recognise this resistance as it does not conform to their ideals. Nevertheless, the demon does not know about her sexual intercourse with other people and therefore feels confident that she is locked away. This suggests that she seems to conform to his rules as she does not challenge his authority in a way that he recognises. However, the novel clarifies the captive is still resistant and therefore in a position where it is not possible to be completely restricted. This mirrors Shahrazad's storytelling when she chooses a position to resist and challenge the king's authority with storytelling, which also means that she has to stay with him throughout. Although this seems to restrict women in a limited space, I would argue that it demonstrates different

---

203 Al-Shaykh, *Nights*, p. 218.

forms of resistance through which women can gain control of their bodies and
voices.

Resembling Shahrazad, the protagonist of the tale of 'The Woman and Her
Five Lovers' sexually manipulates various men of power to access the liberating
space where she is able to overthrow their authority by locking them in a chest
while Shahrazad locks the king in an unending narrative. In doing so, this tale
itself functions as a practice of postcolonial feminine writing in terms of both
its (repetitive and circular) structure and content. It is the story of a woman
who fights for her lover's release from prison. When she petitions for help, she is
propositioned by numerous corrupt people of authority such as the judge and the
mayor. They promise her lover's release on the condition that she has intercourse
with them. She shows her astonishment by exclaiming 'But you're the judge! [...]
if you behave like this, how can you punish others for taking advantage of the
helpless?'[204] This demonstrates that the woman is oppressed by people of a higher
social status. Therefore, she lures each man into her home with the promise of
intercourse, but instead robs them of their clothes and thus the signifiers of their
hierarchical status and locks each one in five different compartments of a chest.
Here, the woman replicates Shahrazad's position in her approach as she uses
her body to operate within the patriarchal systems of power in order to undo
them. Just like Shahrazad, who figuratively locks Shahrayar in her narrative, this
woman indeed locks men away by re-writing her sexuality into a convincing and
captivating narrative. In doing so, she allows the audience/reader to recognise the
potential of re-writing confining gendered power structures. Correspondingly,
I want to analyse to what extent Shahrazad's storytelling opens up a liberating
space for non-conforming bodies.

Bodies (Un)veiled: Narrating Non-conforming Bodies

The *Nights* intimately follows the technique of postcolonial feminine writing in
critically interrogating social norms and how they consequently restrict bodies
within fixed positions. The imposition of societal norms tends to impose gender
codes and demands compliance with these expectations. Postcolonial feminine
writing enables the re-thinking of bodies as different and non-conforming.
Accordingly, the text presents new and creative ways to re-imagine these bodies
and acknowledge/embrace their differences. Postcolonial feminine writing
opens up a liberating space to discuss the fact that bodies as heteronormative and

---

204 Al-Shaykh, *Nights*, p. 220.

conforming may also be challenging and non-conforming. I would suggest that liberating spaces are forms of (un)veiling as some bodies refuse to stay restricted within rigid binary structures and instead assume a disguise that conforms to these structures. This non-conforming and non-heteronormative disguise is powerful because characters are socially recognised by their peers in accordance with their intentions. This gives them the ability and potential to transform these social and gender boundaries from within.

As a typical Shahrazadean technique, this novel particularly focuses on gender non-conforming bodies. The understanding of bodies as heteronormative is unsettled by demonstrating how the corporeal does not easily fit with the gender categories to which it is assigned. In accordance with Shahrazad's narrative voice and style, this novel resists the definitiveness of gender categories. The text presents the character of Abu Nuwas, a castrated poet who works as an entertainer for Haroun al-Rashid to acknowledge a discrepancy between his gender and corporeality. Abu Nuwas describes himself and a eunuch dervish as 'half men'.[205] It is recognised as a performance of wit by Haroun al-Rashid and aimed to be humorous. Precisely because Abu Nuwas delivers this assertion playfully, almost as a second thought, correcting himself 'seven men; no, I mean, six men and two half men', he indeed undermines the predominance of penis as an indication of masculinity.[206] This interaction allows for an interrogation of his gender and sexual identity. Accordingly, his narrative voice is the first hint at establishing a non-heteronormative identity. He recites a poem,

> You assured me that my lover's kisses
> Would sweetly abundant be
> But in return he received but a nasty nip.
> Don't rebuke me, I feel no shame.[207]

The poet clearly addresses his queer partner as the poem recites 'no shame'. Here, his non-heteronormative relationship could provoke a sense of shame as it does not conform to societal gender and sexuality norms. However, he performs his sexual identity with 'no shame' and resists being rebuked for his non-heteronormative desires. The narrative of the poem enables the poet to construct his sexual identity and thus the text allows him to identify his gender identity. This occurs when Abu Nuwas claims that '[w]e men are not crafty and

205 Al-Shaykh, *Nights*, p. 188.
206 Ibid., p. 188.
207 Ibid., p. 97.

wily like women', showing a desire to be part of a group of 'we men'.[208] While this constructs a tension between gender and sex norms, it also implies that he is accepted as a man within his social group and his gender is predominantly based on recognition by his peers. Furthermore, the poet clarifies his sexual identity when he claims '[w]e are men and women and we blame each other. But can we live apart? I could very easily live without the opposite sex, but most of humankind cannot'.[209] Although he seems to construct a binary opposition between men and women, his statement deliberately disrupts the understanding of a binary gender system because his sexuality almost pushes him out of this binary as he lives 'without the opposite sex'. This opens up the potential of rethinking bodies and shows how bodies do not always conform to societal norms surrounding gender.

The novel demonstrates how characters have the potential to re-invent their genders perpetually through the act of (un)veiling. Zumurrud is a female slave who deliberately manipulates her identity as a method of survival. Her identity is established through her class and gender as a woman and slave. Nevertheless, Zumurrud does not conform to her identity boundaries. While she was still a slave, she intentionally challenged her identity as a slave because she repetitively insulted her bidders in a slave market. Zumurrud rejects being sold to 'a decrepit old man [...] barely able to stand [whose] penis will most assuredly be as soft as a piece of dough'.[210] The novel shows that she does not only resist her class identity, but she also resists her gender identity by challenging gender dynamics and the so-called superiority of her bidders. Zumurrud provides the money for her auction secretly to a man of her own choosing, who is poorer than her. She offers the auctioneer her ring in exchange for being sold to the bidder of her choice. Although she is a female slave, I would suggest that the novel deliberately unsettles her position in relation to her bidders as she has money of her own, which is sufficient for her to make a deal with another man. Therefore, I would suggest that she resists being objectified although she is supposed to be a slave and hold no rights. Further, the novel shows how she gains authority by cross-dressing as a man and manipulating her gender identity. Zumurrud falls into a trap, from which she escapes by assuming a masculine form. The fact that she can assume a new identity easily proves that her identity is fluid and malleable. The novel explores the fluidity of gender boundaries as she 'dressed in men's

---

208 Ibid., p. 190.
209 Ibid., p. 229.
210 Al-Shaykh, *Nights*, p. 252.

clothes, wrapped her head in a turban and strapped a sword at her waist, [...] mounted one of the two horses'.[211] Upon her realisation that there are people waiting at a city gate with the custom 'the first man who arrives in the direction from which [she] came is appointed [their] king' after their previous king's death, she manipulates not only her body but also her social class. Zumurrud claims 'in a deep manly voice' that he is no common man with his connections to a noble family that he left behind.[212] Here, the pronoun change from 'she' to 'he' is a deliberate act to recognise his performance of male gender and fluidity of the gender identity. Zumurrud is expected to follow heteronormative social and gender norms to pass as a king. He is pressured by society to take a wife or visit his concubines. He marries a woman fearing that they will discover 'the King is not complete', and here, being complete refers to having a penis.[213] This clearly undermines patriarchal and heteronormative gender norms as it breaks the connection between penis and masculinity. The marriage appears to confirm society's expectations of heteronormativity; however, his marriage is also the act that disrupts heteronormativity. It is precisely because Zumurrud appears to conform to the social norms that she/he is skilfully manipulating them. This is a form of (un)veiling as she/he seems to follow the social rules whilst challenging the very act of a heteronormative marriage. Thus, I would argue that the novel effectively questions the corporeal heteronormativity of bodies. Consequently, the changeability of identity re-defined by cross-dressing provides the potential for her/him to gain access to a voice and position of power. It is a significant position because it demonstrates how gender identity is open to manipulation and keeps the power with the individual. That Zumurrud takes over the patriarchal gender and class system, which previously enslaved her, makes her position more powerful just as Shahrazad gains authority over the narrative. Here, Zumurrud re-writes the restrictive social norms by actively using her body to manipulate the very core of these structures.

The novel also resists one-dimensionality of bodies by re-imagining the potential of hybrid bodies. Hybridity shows how bodies are not readily conforming to heteronormative ideals. For example, the late husband of the mistress of the house is a supernatural character named Azraq Blue, who can exist both as a supernatural creature and as a human being; his identity cannot be reduced to one. The mistress of the house watches a huge bird that shakes until a man

---

211 Ibid., p. 262.
212 Al-Shaykh, *Nights*, p. 262.
213 Ibid., p. 268.

emerges underneath his feathers. She recognises that 'he was not like any other man' not only because he is different, but also because his physical attributes are beautiful, 'as if God had created him to bewitch and enchant'.[214] Enchanted by his beauty, the mistress of the house has intercourse with him: 'what would happen between a man and a woman happened between [them]'.[215] Whilst Azraq Blue is a bird, he is also a man and acts as a human being. The novel clearly shows that Azraq Blue's identity is not reducible to a human being free of his supernatural roots. When he disrobes his feathers, he wishes to hide them because 'these feathers are [his] power and soul' implying that his identity is plural and exists simultaneously with his bird identity.[216] When he discovers that his feathers are damaged and not functioning, he recognises that it will bring about his demise. The mistress of the house insists that he must survive because he has a supernatural body. Azraq Blue falls down on the floor and his wife '[tries] to take him out his feathers, in the hope that he might survive as a man, but inside [she finds] nothing but ashes'.[217] This is a significant point in the novel as it embraces the potential plurality of bodies. Azraq Blue's body cannot be reduced to a human or a bird as he has to embrace his plural selves. He performs plural identities that are inseparable. The external intervention in the plurality of his body destroys him. Therefore, enforcing bodies into a fixed binary position is effectively impossible. Bodies can be plural and even in identifying with a specific form or gender does not negate this plurality.

In re-defining the forms of female and male genitalia as different and specific, the text develops a sense of plurality. Three women in the tale of 'The Porter and the Three Ladies' play a game with the porter. They each expect him to guess the name of their genitalia. The porter replies '[y]our cunt, […] [y]our womb, your clitoris, your hole, your well, your pussy, your slit, your egg factory'.[218] This response firmly mirrors the social construction of women as sexual objects and restrains them in a binary opposition. Whilst the porter clearly attempts to label their sexual organs with pejorative terms that objectify women as sex objects and/or potential mothers, the language of the narrator resists objectification by allowing each woman to re-define themselves by re-naming their genitalia as specific. The shopper renames her genitalia 'the basil that grows on the bridges'

214 Al-Shaykh, *Nights*, p. 142.
215 Ibid., p. 144.
216 Ibid., p. 147.
217 Ibid., p. 152.
218 Al-Shaykh, *Nights*, p. 31.

and mimics her genitalia while addressing the porter.[219] The impersonation of the genitals gives her a plurality within her body. The doorkeeper renames hers 'the husked sesame' and the mistress of the house renames hers 'the inn of Abu Masrur'.[220] Whilst it affirms the plurality of women, it also demonstrates that the novel gives the potential for agency to anyone who can manipulate their bodies. Every time the porter attempts to address their genitals with the same name, he is punished by being slapped and kicked. This torture bears a significant message for the porter, according to Mernissi, that 'it is foolish for a man to pretend to name what only a woman can control – her sex. For men to control what they cannot even adequately name is therefore pure delusion'.[221] As Sellers explains, women's bodies, alongside their sexual experiences, are continuously 'appropriated and determined by men', which needs to be disrupted.[222] Cixous affirms that 'women have almost everything to write about femininity: about their sexuality, […] about the infinite and mobile complexity of their becoming erotic, […] discoveries of a formerly timid region'.[223] Previously unrecognised feminine sexuality must be brought into the text as Cixous theorises because it is not one-dimensional, it is plural, and it is not uniform, it is complex. As Cixous urges, women should discover the initially reticent region of their bodies. The novel therefore keeps re-inventing bodies alongside recognising female genitalia for its own signification and thus transforming the position of women as a binary to men. Here, it is the recognition of the clitoris as a part of the female genitalia that further prevents the woman from simply being a sex object for the others' desire. It is a celebration of woman's difference. Furthermore, the novel keeps the association between the body and the word with a reference to the female genitalia as it is a clear digression from the mainstream narrative discourse. The position of women controlling their own bodies and desires proves significant when the porter is similarly allowed to re-define his penis as 'the smashing mule'.[224] Here, the novel does not simply elevate women's social and gender position, but it indicates the potential of the infinite choices and possibilities in allowing women to explore their own bodies and sexualities. It is not only women who emerge as powerful out of this exchange, but men as well. Therefore, I would

---

219 Ibid., p. 32.
220 Ibid., p. 32.
221 Mernissi, *Scheherazade*, pp. 67–8.
222 Susan Sellers, *Language and Sexual Difference: Feminist Writing in France* (New York: MacMillan Education, 1991), p. 75.
223 Cixous, 'Sorties', p. 94.
224 Al-Shaykh, *Nights*, p. 33.

suggest that the very understanding of postcolonial feminine writing aims to destabilise patriarchal social and gender norms. In doing so, it allows a re-definition of power dynamics between masculinity and society. While the novel demonstrates that it is possible to be plural and hybrid within a body, it also shows how the potential of transformation in social and gender norms lies in the notion of (un)veiling by seeming to conform to these norms whilst intimately re-writing them.

Conclusion

This chapter has argued that al-Shaykh's *Nights* is itself a form of postcolonial feminine writing while also re-telling long-standing Shahrazadean tales. Shahrazad is a significant figure as a narrator whom contemporary postcolonial writers return to and revive. I have argued that understanding the multiple layers of Shahrazad's existence allows for a better understanding of postcolonial feminine writing as Shaharazad establishes an undeniable link between the body and the narrative. al-Shaykh specifically provides Shahrazad with the potential to transform the status quo of patriarchal literary discourse. Rather than simply replicating the tales, this novel functions as a subversive re-narrative in allowing marginalised characters and narrators the ability to gain a voice and a recognised position in storytelling. The text itself functions as a form of postcolonial feminine writing by 'making it possible' for Shahrazad and other narrators to gain access to a voice.

This novel intervenes in restrictive power structures and re-imagines them. The text is concerned with how sexual desire becomes the basis of resistance for multiple characters. By bringing together people from various social class backgrounds, the novel attempts to disturb the so-called power of the patriarchal authority. Even before Shahrazad herself becomes a part of the tales, the text demonstrates instances of disrupting social and gendered norms. The notion of resistance to the patriarchal authority clearly relies on the practice of sexual desire. Several characters adopt the form of (un)veiling to create a disguise through which they appear to conform and remain reliable. However, the very technique of (un)veiling transforms these social norms and hierarchies as repetition of this disguise is subversive and non-conforming. Moreover, the text demonstrates how Shahrazad's narrative intertwines sexual desire with narrative desire, allowing the narrator to continue her storytelling for an indefinite period because the text suggests the potential of narrative as a means of confining the patriarchal authority within an imaginary 'chest'. This is particularly significant because she takes risks when she begins a new tale or when she stops narrating.

The final section has argued that postcolonial feminine writing allows for re-imagining bodies as non-conforming and divergent. The text shows how different forms of pluralities and hybridity are possible. In doing so, the novel problematizes the understanding of corporeal heteronormativity. It is a very Shahrazadean technique to use the form of (un)veiling as a subversive disguise. I have suggested that the potential of plurality allows the interrogation of patriarchal literary discourse and the practice of gender roles is repeatedly undermined in the novel as a result. The text uses these gender codes to its advantage all the while subverting them. Moreover, bodies are re-imagined as multiple and hybrid, demonstrating the impossibility of reducing bodies to a single unit. Indeed, bodies are already multiple and do not readily conform to societal norms. It is specifically a postcolonial feminine trait that the text demonstrates the plurality of female and male genitalia. That is, the text resists the patriarchal determination of sex by recognising their individualities and differences. It allows for men as well as women to re-define their identities without patriarchal imposition.

Having analysed multiple and hybrid bodies in this chapter, the next chapter will analyse the tension between non-conforming bodies (e.g. the fat body and the dwarf) and the gaze in Shafak's *The Gaze* (2006). Al-Shaykh adopts and rewrites the tales from the *Nights* in this novel whilst Shafak closely follows narrative form and techniques in *The Gaze*. I will further my argument, positing that postcolonial feminine writing re-creates liberating spaces for women's narrative voices whilst demonstrating how postcolonial feminine writing also re-imagines multiple positions of the gaze.

Chapter II: 'A Unique World of Spectacle': Re- formulating the Gaze in Shafak's *The Gaze* (2006)

Introduction

With a focus on Elif Shafak's *The Gaze* (2006), this chapter will investigate how Shafak's literary claim on Shahrazadean identity, evidenced through her story-telling, transforms Shafak's narrative by liberating it from male-dominated, linear narrative boundaries.[225] More specifically, I will explore the ways in which the gaze constructs and deconstructs identity. Building on al-Shaykh's Shahrazadean narrative style in *1001 Nights*, this chapter will argue that *The Gaze* challenges the dominant male gaze with multiple gazing positions as well as multiple narrative layers. This deconstruction of the dominant gaze by multiple gazes works to destabilise identity and proves to be liberating for the characters in the novel in imaginative ways. This is a significant aspect of the novel because Shafak clearly re-creates the position of Shahrazad when she steals the gaze from the dominant position of the male gaze and re-imagines it in her own words. In addition, the novel follows Shahrazad's tradition of storytelling, as I explore with the concept of postcolonial feminine writing, by tracing the potential of voice back to a woman's body through multiple gazing positions. Indeed, the gaze becomes a tool (such as the veil) through which the text posits liberation and agency. I argue that the novel articulates marginalised bodies through various gazing positions and seizes the potential of liberation, not only for women, but also for other marginalised figures. Specifically, I will explore how Shahrazad's narrative is embedded in the repetition of form and content and how this act of repetition is manifested in Shafak's exploration of the gaze to interrogate the boundaries of identity. By way of subversive repetition, I suggest that Shafak opens up the potential for creating liberating spaces. Similar to Shahrazad's narrative, Shafak's authorial voice is powerful in the novel as she creates layers of narrative and

---

225 This novel is originally published in Turkish as Elif Şafak, *Mahrem* (Istanbul: Metis Yayinlari, 1999). It is first published in English as *The Gaze* by Marion Boyars Publishers in 2006. I will be referring to 2010 Penguin edition: Elif Shafak, *The Gaze*, trans. by Brendan Freely (London: Penguin, 2010).

multiple voices, which often echo the voice of those who are usually marginalised and silenced.

The Gaze resembles al-Shaykh's *Nights* in both narrative content and style. Shafak writes two stories about the concept of the gaze and constructs them with a similar structure to Shahrazad's tales. These stories revolve around how looking constructs social norms and is also, in turn, constructed by social norms. Thus, Shafak's stories in the novel portray the dominant gaze while simultaneously undermining that gaze. In an interview, Shafak says that *The Gaze* is 'a conscious reinterpretation of the narrative tradition of *One Thousand and One Nights*'.[226] Therefore, I suggest that Shafak not only re-interprets the *Nights*, but also writes in a style that I am calling postcolonial feminine writing. Postcolonial feminine writing builds on the patriarchal literary discourse that has been previously denied to women. As I discussed in my Introduction, Cixous urges women to claim the right to their bodies and bring them back into writing so that their bodies are heard. Along similar lines, Fanon discusses the significance of Algerian women in their use of (un)veiling in the line of national liberation and that this creates a great potential for gendered liberation as well. Similarly, Shafak re-writes the gaze with Shahrazadean narrative techniques, 'to make it hers, containing it, taking it in her own mouth, biting that tongue with her very own teeth to invent for herself a language to get inside of'.[227] Shafak writes the novel with the understanding of different possibilities to re-tell her stories in a language that she invented (such as Dictionary of Gazes) and she admits that she 'told stories within stories and then destroyed them one by one' with their own negations.[228] This description relates to the structure of Shahrazad's storytelling because Shahrazad organises her tales in a clear order with a pedagogical intention for her audience. Likewise, Shafak presents her stories not in a chronological order, but in an order that challenges the reader to re-consider their perceptions of social categories such as gender and class. Postcolonial feminine writing therefore is the theoretical framework that allows for a reading of this text as reclaiming a literary space that gives embodied voice to marginalised peoples.

The novel begins with a frame story that appears to be irrelevant to the subsequent stories in the novel. Contrary to Shahrazad's storytelling, Shafak begins the frame story with a first-person narrator and subsequent stories are narrated

---

226 Myriam J.A. Chancy, 'Migrations: A Meridians Interview with Elif Shafak', *Meridians*, 4, 1 (2003), pp. 55–85, p. 73.

227 Cixous, 'Medusa', p. 887.

228 Chancy, 'Migrations', p. 73.

with an omniscient narrator. The shift to the omniscient narrator indicates a deliberate intention to distance the reader from the narrator's perspective and re-tell her story in an imagined space and time. This switch in narrative voice bears striking resemblance to Shahrazad, who assumes voices of different narrators to distance her voice. Likewise, Shafak employs the same narrative technique to create a liberating space to make the narrative 'hers'. The frame story is narrated by an unnamed narrator, who focuses on her fat body and her relationship with her dwarf partner B-C, taking place in contemporary Istanbul. They become the point of focus as a couple for other characters in the novel. While the narrator is highly agitated and attempts to evade the looks of others, B-C seeks the gaze deliberately by posing as a nude model for art students. B-C utilises and thereby reflects the gaze back to the others by initially modelling and later compiling a 'Dictionary of Gazes', in which he re-defines words in relation to looking. Stories in the novel seem disconnected because links between the stories and narrators are not clarified in a way that is similar to Shahrazad's narrative of a story-within-story. The second story appears to be a re-narration of B-C's compilation, which is set in nineteenth-century Istanbul and about Keramet Keske Mumi Memis Efendi, who is born with a 'virtually transparent [face]. His mouth-nose-eyebrows-eyes were both complete and incomplete' and that makes him a victim to the dominant normative gaze.[229] Since he feels uncomfortable being looked at as a creature of wonder, he builds two tents which offer 'a unique world of spec-tacle', displaying beauty for male spectators in one tent, ugliness for women in the other.[230] His act intends to mirror the gaze back to the spectators. The simi-larities between B-C and Keramet are connected by the theme of the gaze.

The plot is historically and geographically cyclical beginning in late twentieth-century Istanbul and developing with stories from seventeenth-century Siberia, nineteenth-century France, nineteenth-century Istanbul and returning to the story of twentieth-century Istanbul, which breaks the linearity of narration.[231] The setting of the novel, contemporary Istanbul, is significant as it is 'nei-ther completely familiar nor completely foreign, neither entirely Eastern nor Western'.[232] This indicates a position of transition between the East and the West.

---

229 Shafak, *The Gaze*, p. 34. I will refer to this character as Keramet.
230 Ibid., p. 123.
231 The novel's narrative of late nineteenth century Istanbul makes several references to colonial expeditions showing the Ottoman's fascination with the West and Westernisation.
232 Donna Landry, 'Queer Islam and New Historicism', *Cultural Studies*, 25, 2 (2011), pp. 147–63, p. 152.

It allows the novel to be constructed through ideas of fluidity and multiplicity, which are explored by imagining several gazes different from the dominant male gaze. The novel frequently relies on the unsettling influence of different gazes, which suggests an imaginative type of gazing without definite boundaries. Thus, I would argue that the novel challenges the hierarchy of the gaze by refusing to restrict the setting to a single historical and national location, and this indicates Shafak's tension with nationhood and her recognition of multiplicity of gazes.[233] Moreover, the text can reclaim the position that the male gaze initially denied to women and liberates the gaze from the dominant boundaries of the male gaze by destabilising it historically, geographically and nationally. The novel therefore revolves around the characters that tend to be objects of the dominant male gaze although it does not limit their positions to objects. Rather, characters occupy positions of active looking, which indicates Shafak's negotiation of identity positions and shows the shift in the power of looking.

Before moving on with my discussion of the novel, I want to focus on how other critics deal with Shafak's *The Gaze*. Reflecting its name, the novel has specifically been addressed in relation to the concept of the gaze by Zeynep Z. Atayurt-Fenge. She discusses how Shafak successfully 'merges' Western and Eastern narrative traditions.[234] She argues that Shafak draws circles in her novel, which reproduces the same stories differently and that this serves a political aim 'to critique the implications of the gaze cross-culturally and historically'.[235] She points out that the novel reverses the gaze and allows the fat woman to 'derive a certain subversive pleasure that has been denied to her as a fat woman'.[236] Even though my literary analysis of the novel runs along similar lines to Atayurt-Fenge, I contextualise how Shafak continuously re-invents the gaze through her imaginative style, and in doing so Shafak demonstrates a writing style that I am naming postcolonial feminine writing. By drawing clear links between Shafak's narrative and Shahrazad's storytelling, I demonstrate how Shafak undoes various

233 The text describes the face of La Belle Annabelle as impossible to geographically situate because '[it] belonged to neither West nor East' (p. 152) even though she is of Western origin. Shafak's engagement with West and East as inseparable demonstrates a fluidity of identity instead of rigid national and racial boundaries.
234 Zeynep Z. Atayurt-Fenge, ' "This is a World of Spectacles": Cyclical Narratives and Circular Visionary Formations in Elif Shafak's *The Gaze*', *Critique: Studies in Contemporary Fiction*, 58, 3 (2017), pp. 287–99, p. 289.
235 Ibid., p. 296.
236 Ibid., p. 295.

gender and social norms giving a voice and gaze to marginalised figures insofar as they become the subjects of the gaze.

Although the title of the novel calls for a focus on the concept of the gaze, the novel can be interrogated in other ways. For instance, Nese Demirci stresses the fact that Shafak does not randomly select the names of the characters. Rather, Shafak benefits from 'the symbolic power of names' and it is important to understand the function of these names 'to understand the overall meaning of the text'.[237] Demirci shows how the names in Shafak's various novels symbolise change insofar as the characters either opt to change their names or question their identities through their names. She also points out that Shafak opts to leave the narrator of *The Gaze* unnamed and to scatter her character across all time and space.[238] Building on this idea, I would suggest that the novel refuses to confine the narrator by any narrative or normative limitations. Although I do not specifically question why the narrator is unnamed, I concentrate on how the narrator is constantly re-imagined through different characters, and how it therefore becomes difficult to confine her identity within pre-defined social and gender boundaries.

In a different context, Donna Landry analyses how Shafak queers the gaze and contextualises the novel with queer theory and new historicism. Landry argues that Shafak engages with 'a history of sexuality in which a Western grid of heteronormativity slips, fails to fit the scene' even if the author does not particularly set out to represent queer characters.[239] For Landry, the fat woman is represented as a queer character as she 'violates' gender norms and 'transgresses' femininity.[240] I agree with Landry's interpretations of the text insofar as the novel indicates a transgression of gender and sexuality. However, Landry does not recognise that the novel posits a shift of power within the fat woman's body, able to perform different gender roles by presenting a disguise. I explore how disguise allows the fat woman to shift the power dynamics whilst undermining the controlling gaze.

This novel was first published in Turkish with the title, *Mahrem* (1999), which means the private. The Turkish title refers to the exclusive space of the harem because the harem is almost always known for its exclusivity for women and

---

237 Nese Demirci, 'Symbolism of Names in Elif Shafak's Pinhan, Araf and Mahrem', *Turkish Studies*, 5, 3 (2010), pp. 996–1008, p. 997. As this article is written in Turkish except the abstract, which is written in English, the references to this article are my own translation.

238 Ibid., p. 1007.

239 Landry, 'Queer Islam', p. 148.

240 Ibid., p. 160.

its restriction on the unauthorised looks of men. Both titles indicate a tension between looking, gender, privacy and society by pointing out the significance of the gaze in constructing individual and social identity. This tension proves to be subversive just as the veil proves to be subversive in postcolonial feminine writing with its performative qualities which allow for the dominant codes of looking to be interrogated and destabilised. E. Ann Kaplan argues, 'looking relations are never innocent' since they almost always construct social and gender stereo- types.[241] These stereotypes constantly reproduce gender norms and maintain heteronormativity, thereby containing marginalised peoples within a patriarchal discourse that obliterates their voices. Therefore, I suggest societal norms should be re-imagined and thus seeking the potential for women's voices. Accordingly, I re-formulate the gaze within the theoretical framework of postcolonial femi- nine writing as a positionality of looking that is perpetually re-defined. I argue that Shafak re-constructs the gaze to explore its boundaries as she invents for herself a gaze in the language she can 'get inside of'. This posits seeking voice and agency as embodied looking and a mask/disguise deflecting the dominant positions of the gaze and allowing for the object to also be a subject of the gaze.

Jacques Lacan contends that the gaze is formative to identity.[242] Lacan focuses on identity formation and psychosexual development in relation to the gaze. He divides psychosexual development into the realms of the Imaginary and the Symbolic. Throughout the Imaginary stage, the child learns to see and recognise itself (initially through the eyes of the mother and then the mirror), which begins the formation of the self. Lacan says: '[I]n the scopic field, the gaze is outside, I am looked at, that is to say, I am a picture'.[243] He suggests that the gaze is not

241 E. Ann Kaplan, *Looking for the Other: Feminism, Film and the Imperial Gaze* (London and New York: Routledge, 1997), p. 6.

242 Laura Mulvey's 'Visual Pleasure and Narrative Cinema' is foundational in terms of defining the male gaze from a cinematic perspective. Mulvey formulates this con- cept of the male gaze based on Freudian and Lacanian psychoanalysis. Although I recognise Mulvey's undeniable influence in various theories of the gaze, I choose to not include her in my own analyses of the gaze due to her extensive focus on women's passivity within this hierarchy of the male gaze. However, I opt to draw on Lacan in constructing my argument on the gaze, because Lacan proposes 'a funda- mental structure in the ways in which the subject relates to the cultural order [and] in which subjectivity itself is formed through [its] mechanisms'. Patrick Fuery and Nick Mansfield, *Cultural Studies and the New Humanities: Concepts and Controversies* (Melbourne: Oxford UP, 1997), p 70.

243 Jacques Lacan, *Book XI: The Four Fundamental Concepts of Psychoanalysis* (New York and London: W. W. Norton & Company, 1981, repr. 1998), p. 106.

confined to the boundaries of a subject; rather, the gaze provides the perception of the self from an external perspective and therefore gives the sense of an image. The picture's proximity or distance determines the influence of the gaze. Lacan writes,

> What determines me, at the most profound level, in the visible, is the gaze that is outside. It is through the gaze that I enter light and it is from the gaze that I receive its effects. Hence it comes about that the gaze is the instrument through which light is embodied and through which [...] I am *photo-graphed*.[244]

Lacan argues that the gaze is an *instrument* that works to form identity. Here, it is the look of the outside world through which we come to recognise ourselves and the outside world. The subject is formed through social recognition and sight. Thus, the gaze here defines the object of the look precisely by en-lightening it. When the subject is *photo-graphed* by others, the subject is able to solidify their understanding of their identity as the other perceives them. As Beth Newman points out '[t]hough another's look can be experienced as threatening – as a bid for mastery or an assertion of power – [...] the other's look is also necessary to one's sense of self'.[245] Thus, the gaze is an *assertion* of the autonomy of the subject, but it is also significant for the object of the look because identity formation, to a certain extent, depends on the recognition of the self by the others.

   To be able to frame the gaze within postcolonial feminine writing, we need to re-interpret the hierarchical position of 'the gaze' where the male gaze is assumed to be dominant. By manipulating the position of the male gaze, the potential for agency is posited on the body. The body plays a significant role in how gender norms are manifested and therefore it is essential to re-claim the body in a position of looking that is not already restrained by dominant codes of looking. Shafak writes in a way that follows Cixous's exclamation: '[w]rite your self. Your body must be heard'.[246] Shafak does not only write to be read and heard, but she almost re-interprets Cixous's urging as if 'your body' must be looked at and seen, and thus 'the woman [...] takes on an intrinsic value as a woman in her own eyes and, undeniably, acquires body and sex'.[247] With this gesture, Shafak proposes how the gaze is significant for identification of the self to acquire her body and gender in 'her own eyes'. As I argued earlier in this chapter, the gaze in

---

244 Ibid., p. 106.
245 Beth Newman, 'Getting Fixed: Feminine Identity and Scopic Crisis in *The Turn of the Screw*', *Novel*, 26, 1 (1992), pp. 43–63, p. 45.
246 Cixous, 'Medusa', p. 880.
247 Ibid., p. 891.

postcolonial feminine writing can be framed as a concept of looking that subverts dominant gazes since it is re-defined by not only presenting negotiable positions of the gaze but positions of the subject as well. Laura U. Marks imagines a different gaze for women in a queer setting which is liberating not only for women, but men as well. Marks claims that the gay club scene provides 'a voyeuristic feast for a woman who wants to look at men, or to *learn* to look at men, without the look back'.[248] Deviating from other discussions of the male gaze, Marks intends to look at men as objects and opens the possibility of changing the position of the gaze along with the subject of the gaze. She finds the earlier homoerotic look in straight cinema problematic since 'in addition to being male, [the gaze] is still dominating, penetrating'. She argues that for women to align with this type of look is to maintain the patriarchal gaze, which continues to operate as restrictively as before. Developing Kaja Silverman's arguments that suggest 'men are just as specular (and as powerless) as women are', Marks considers the elimination of the hierarchy of the gaze suggested by Silverman because 'it would seem that there is *no* erotic way to look at the male body, since to make it the object of the gaze is simultaneously to deflate it, to castrate it, make it undesirable. According to this view, just as I get the opportunity to look, my object is seized from me!'[249] Thus, Marks suggests that eliminating the male gaze is not a solution for destabilising the female gaze. This suggests that women would still be rendered powerless since they would have no power to look, and therefore they would never be subjects of the gaze. Instead, Marks offers a model of spectatorship that is defined in terms of the sexual practice of S/M. She explains her use of 'S/M' as a bedroom practice of playing dominant/submissive roles rather than sadomasochism, which she defines as a psychoanalytic condition. The practice of S/M becomes a mode of defining positions based on relational roles.

Marks explains that S/M is 'the limited, contractual relation in which two people consent to play out a fantasy relationship'.[250] However, she does not theorise the roles of S/M as rigid positions. Instead, Marks argues,

> [I]n an S/M-style erotic look there is a fluidity of movement between these positions. To recognize the contingency of power on position makes it possible to enjoy the privileges of power in a limited way. [...] Domination is a necessary part of erotic relations. [T]

248 Laura U. Marks, *Touch: Sensuous Theory and Multisensory Media* (Minneapolis, MN: The University of Minnesota Press, 2002), p. 73.
249 Marks, *Touch*, p. 75.
250 Ibid., p. 77.

here can be no erotic relation when there is an *utter* division of subject and object. [V]
isual eroticism plays with *relations* of looking.[251]

By bringing S/M into the theory of the gaze, she argues that it is possible to
create a setting that allows the dominant and submissive roles to operate in a
fully consensual environment. The roles in an S/M setting are developed as fluid
and enabling. The position of the dominant is just as limited as that of the submissive. By avoiding clear-cut roles, Marks suggests that it is also possible to
change the position of looking just as it is possible to change the roles in S/M: 'a
viewer can make a pact with *many* viewing situations'.[252] Thus, the power does
not belong to a rigid position; rather, the power is experienced in *relations*. It
is dynamic and changing. By discussing the possibility of changing the position and the subject(s) of the gaze, Marks re-appropriates the gaze, creating a
mobile and non-hierarchical mode of looking. Moreover, Marks does not disregard the hierarchy that the gaze provides, instead she re-interprets it to convey
the changeability of the power dynamics. As proposed by Marks, the gaze needs
to be re-woven in terms other than those of the rigid power structures. This is
echoed in postcolonial feminine writing since the key aspect of the concept is to
re-define notions of liberation 'to make it theirs' rather than maintaining patriarchal norms of writing and the gaze. It allows hierarchy to be still maintained, but
it does not confine the power to a specific group of people because it recognises
the possibility of different positions of looking. As in postcolonial feminine
writing, the gaze is re-imagined in this context to liberate voice. This is apparent
in how the text posits the body in narrative and the re-positioning of the gaze.
While exploring boundaries of the gaze, the text interrogates the boundaries of
the body and imagines ways to exist without being defined by the penetrating
gaze of the others. The novel re-creates the narrator in different bodies across
history and offers her the potential to test the boundaries of her own body as
well as her own gaze. When her body is re-contextualised without its restrictive
boundaries, the text allows for her voice to be heard. The narrator is able to share
her own experiences of being the object of the gaze and develops a position as
the subject of the gaze through this re-imagining. Thus, I would argue that the
gaze can be constructed as dynamic, and still powerful.

As Marks posits different positions of looking, I want to suggest the novel offers
the potential for women to 'fly away' from rigid power structures. By 'stealing' the
right to gaze, women are able to have authority over their own bodies and voices.

---

251 Ibid., p. 77.
252 Marks, *Touch*, p. 88.

Here, flying, a concept central to postcolonial feminine writing, is formulated as women's gesture by Cixous because '[women have] been able to possess anything only by flying; [they] lived in flight, stealing away, finding, when desired, narrow passageways, hidden crossovers'.[253] Cixous suggests that women learn to steal or fly away as techniques of 'dislocating things and values'.[254] Flight becomes almost as significant as 'stealing' in 'disorienting' the patriarchal discourse, because it offers an escape from the patriarchal systems of power by uncovering 'hidden crossovers'. I would suggest that these passageways not only indicate transition, but they also connote fluidity and a refusal to be captured by the dominant male gaze. Thus, flight can also be empowering, albeit temporary and 'narrow'. In addition, Cixous recognises the significance of the gaze in power structures and also challenges the earlier positions of the female gaze defined in relation to the male gaze. To quote Cixous,

> She doesn't watch herself, she doesn't measure herself, she doesn't examine herself, not the image, not the copy. [S]he who doesn't watch herself, doesn't reappropriate all images reflected in people's faces, is not the devourer of eyes. She who looks with the look that recognizes, that studies, respects, doesn't take, doesn't claw, but attentively, with gentle relentlessness, contemplates and reads, caresses, bathes, makes the other gleam. Brings back to light the life that's been buried, fugitive, made too prudent.[255]

Cixous refutes the idea of women as an image, as a copy that is constructed by the male gaze. Thus, women should not be measured or examined by the standards of the male gaze. Cixous here develops a powerful woman by defining her as a being who is not re-appropriating her image based on how she is seen, but who becomes the one to look, to recognise differences and make them visible. Cixous discusses that she does not become the erotic/fetishist object of the male gaze when she evades this re-appropriation of the self through the look of the other. She looks at herself with a look that recognises her differences that have previously been buried. The gaze here works to bring woman back to light because she does not read her image within the limiting discourse of the male gaze. Similar to her manifesto in 'Medusa' in which she steers women into writing and seizing the means of writing, here she suggests a 'gentle' stubbornness where she resists by developing a new gaze that echoes 'Medusa' in bringing the forbidden back into context. When the subject embodies the look that *recognises*, Cixous suggests

---

253 Cixous, 'Medusa', p. 887.

254 Ibid., p. 887.

255 Hélène Cixous, *Coming to Writing and Other Essays*, ed. by Deborah Jenson, trans. by Sarah Cornell and others (Cambridge, MA: Harvard UP, 1991), p. 51.

that it is possible to contemplate a new gaze that is stripped of its boundaries. Developing this new gaze is possible by always critiquing and questioning the essence of the heteronormative binary within which it was previously situated. While it is not easy to completely dispose of the normative boundaries of the male gaze, this critical interrogation and hence re-definition of the embodied self provides the potential for unsettling its authoritative position. Bringing this new gaze into writing opens up for the space to interrogate the narrative and representational boundaries. While she questions in which ways the gaze works to define bodies and identities, she also questions how the gaze can be re-imagined if re-written in different contexts.

The Oriental gaze bears striking resemblance to the male gaze in how it is usually constructed in binary terms and aims to render the Orient powerless. Said theorises the Oriental gaze as the West's construction of the East in a limited space as he discusses how '[Orientals were] analyzed not as citizens, or even people, but as problems to be solved or confined'.[256] Said portrays the oriental gaze as structuring the East as a still object that is always defined within a confined space. A. K. Ramakrishnan argues that 'generating knowledge requires the knower to identify and speak about an object'.[257] Therefore, it is considered necessary that the self shall deal with an object to produce the knowledge of both the self and the other. However, Ramakrishnan considers the self/other dichotomy as 'a relationship of contextualities rather than distant and neutral entities'.[258] Reflecting on Ramakrishnan, I would argue that the production of knowledge is rather reflexive and shared, although the West has legitimised his pre-given authority by producing knowledge over 'his' other. Thus, 'if the orient is frozen temporally and spatially for the advantage of the West [to gaze and restructure], the Western subject positions itself outside time and space'.[259] This suggests that the position of the West is also contextualised in relation to a 'frozen' other and when the East is taken out of the 'frozen' context, the authority of the West is questionable. This tends to suggest that the West enters into this knowledge-production as similarly vulnerable since the West's positionality depends on an imaginary 'frozen' or rather, to return to Lacan's logic, a *photo-graphed* other. Similarly, women are defined in a restrained space by the male gaze. However, as

---

256 Edward Said, *Orientalism* (New York: Vintage Books, 1978, 1979), p. 207.
257 A.K. Ramakrishnan, 'The Gaze of Orientalism: Reflections on Linking Postcolonialism and International Relations', *International Studies*, 36 (1999), pp. 129–63, p. 132.
258 Ibid., p. 133.
259 Ramakrishnan, 'The Gaze of Orientalism', p. 134.

explored with the Oriental gaze, the boundaries of women as frozen would suggest a re-interpretation of the male gaze as well. Because the position of the male gaze would not be stable, it calls for a re-imagination of the hierarchy of the gaze based on relational positionality.

The discourse of the veil is crucial to postcolonial feminine writing as it demonstrates that non-Western women could re-define themselves by using the colonial tool of unveiling against authorities. For the discussion of the veil, I focus on Meyda Yeğenoğlu who interrogates the essentialism of the Oriental gaze.[260] Questioning the essence of Western identity, Yeğenoğlu argues '[o]ne is not a Western subject because there exists a pre-given structure called the Western culture. [...] One "becomes" and is made Western by being subjected to a process called Westernizing'.[261] As the very project of Westernising depends on the success of performing 'Western', it can be potentially undermined by repeating this performance differently. Therefore, the Western identity is also produced as a part of the negotiation for identity and that makes its authority powerful, but still questionable. Yeğenoğlu discusses how the figure of the 'veiled Oriental woman' is not only a referent for the non-Western woman, but a construction of the Orient as the feminine other, 'always veiled, seductive, and dangerous'.[262] As I discussed in my Introduction, Fanon considers the veil as a significant enabler for Algerian women to navigate through colonial and cultural borders. The veil manipulates the idea of an absolute 'Oriental' woman and is manipulated by women with the creative use of it. Thus, the veil is a crucial notion in postcolonial feminine writing because it becomes a mask that can and shall be worn and removed with regards to the fluctuating context of national liberation and therefore allows the potential for women's agency. Yeğenoğlu further explains that 'since the veil prevents the colonial gaze from attaining such a visibility and hence mastery, its lifting [for the Western subject] becomes essential'.[263] Although Yeğenoğlu suggests that the Western inquiry into the veil turns it into a mask 'behind which the other is suspected of hiding some dangerous secret threatening his unity and stability', Fanon repeatedly argues that it is the repeated practice of (un)veiling by non-Western women that gives them the power over the Western gaze.[264] I would therefore suggest that the veil is a technique of disguise

---

260 Meyda Yeğenoğlu, *Colonial Fantasies: Towards a Feminist Reading of Orientalism* (Cambridge: Cambridge UP, 1998, repr. 2001).
261 Ibid., p. 4.
262 Yeğenoğlu, *Colonial Fantasies*, p. 11.
263 Ibid., p. 12.
264 Ibid., p. 58.

in the novel because (un)veiling challenges and subverts the gaze directed at it without the looker's knowledge. Likewise, the novel shows how different forms of disguise are used to penetrate social norms. Therefore, (un)veiling as disguise becomes a successful tool for transgressing social and gendered boundaries in the novel. Algerian women successfully alter the meaning of the veil within changing contexts: '[w]hat the colonial gaze saw in the Algerian women's disturbing mimicry was a displacement of its own representation of the veil. Hence what once was familiar and recognizable as concealment, mask, masquerading, has now become unfamiliar [and] disturbing'.[265] Here, the veil is not only the border for inside and outside; rather, the veil is scrutinised as both the border for gender [of Algerian women and men] and race [of Algerian women and Western women and men]. It is the reworking of the veil as a deflector of the gaze that is remarkably subversive. While the veil is re-created in a new context that becomes unfamiliar, its shifting position becomes resistant to and undefinable for the Western gaze. However, Yeğenoğlu argues that the veil does not become automatically subversive once it is utilised creatively. Instead, it gains a subversive quality provided that 'the naturalized gender codes are critically reflected upon'.[266] These pre-defined gender norms need to be re-imagined as different within the male-dominant discourse to open up the space for further interrogation. The text shows that the disguise becomes a successful tool when it aims to undermine social and gender roles. Therefore, by using various disguises (either crossdressing or changing social class roles), the characters appear to conform to the dominant gender roles while simultaneously destabilising these norms. (Un) veiling is repeated and therefore becomes a gendered and racialised act of liberation that is forged through postcolonial feminine writing. The act of repetition re-imagines (un)veiling in the context of gazing and thus I analyse how repetition is made manifest in the text in the following section.

Repetition as a Shahrazadean Narrative Technique

Repetition is a significant narrative device in Shahrazad's storytelling and thus *The Gaze*. Etsuko Aoyagi explores repetitiveness in the *Nights* and argues that repetition comes forth as an important element in both the storytelling and the translation of the tales. Translators and re-writers of the *Nights* either find repetition as a 'generative' force and prefer to re-iterate this element or exclude it by

---

265 Yeğenoğlu, *Colonial Fantasies*, p. 65.
266 Ibid., p. 65.

considering it 'a fault, [and] a wasteful and tedious matter'.[267] Sandra Naddaff, also working on the repetition in Shahrazad's storytelling, argues that '[T]he *1001 Nights* is premised upon a fundamental act of repetition. Not only Shahrazad's narrative and sexual activity repeated nightly; it also results in the perpetuation of Shahrayar's royal line, his extension, his repetition of himself in time through his progeny.'[268] Thus, repetition is key to understanding Shahrazad's storytelling and it gives the sense of a circular narrative. As previously discussed in the chapter introduction, Fanon suggests that (un)veiling was a repeated gendered practice in colonial Algeria which transformed colonial and gender dynamics. Similarly, Butler discusses the significance of repetition in gendered and sexed norms:

> [G]aps and fissures are opened up as the constitutive instabilities in such constructions [as gender and sex], as that which escapes or exceeds the norm, as that which cannot be wholly defined or fixed by the repetitive labor of that norm. This instability is the *de*constituting possibility in the very process of repetition, the power that undoes the very effects by which [gender] is stabilised.[269]

Butler suggests that norms are not always repeated entirely and instead at times reveal repetition through gaps or fissures. This suggests that the repeated version of the norm with gaps is the means through which the norm itself is undone and destabilised. Here, this is evident along the lines of why Shafak aims to desta- bilise her narrative with the repetition of the same stories with contradicting conclusions. Repetition strengthens Shafak's narrative voice by reiterating the same story in different contexts. I would therefore suggest Shafak repeats the narrative form and content to strengthen the position of the stories, narrative voice and gaze. Repetition thus results in the creation of an altered form of embodiment as well as an altered way of imagining the form of storytelling.

Repetition is in effect most obvious in the case of child abuse in the novel. Here, repetition works to overcome the sexual trauma in the child's life. Similarly, Shahrazad repeats stories, characters and expressions to help the king overcome his trauma from witnessing his wife's infidelity. Both the king in Shahrazad's storytelling and the child in the novel suffer from trauma that revolves around

---

267 Etsuko Aoyagi, 'Repetitiveness in the *Arabian Nights*: Openness as Self-Foundation', in *The Arabian Nights and Orientalism*, ed. by Yuriko Yamanaka and Tetsuo Nishio (I.B. Tauris: London and New York, 2006), p. 70.

268 Sandra Naddaff, *Arabesque: Narrative Structure and the Aesthetics of Repetition in 1001 Nights* (Evanston, IL: Northwestern UP, 1991), p. 59.

269 Judith Butler, *Bodies That Matter* (London and New York: Routledge, 1993, 2011), p. xix, emphasis in original.

sexual violence, despite obvious differences. Shafak follows Shahrazad's narrative in validating the incident based on witnessing. The incident is proven to be true based on the king's brother's witnessing, which provokes more anguish and violence for the king. The child however similarly searches for witnesses for the abuse and questions the gaze of their landlady's cat and the divine gaze: 'Elsa [the cat] had seen everything […] she shouldn't have seen. […] She became confused. If only she could find a way to climb over the clouds, she could ask God whether or not he'd seen what happened in the coal shed'.[270] The child believes '[i]f there are no witnesses a person can forget the past'.[271] Although the child cannot interrogate or punish the divine gaze, she punishes the cat in a similar way to the king, who punishes all women for his wife's infidelity. The cat is found bloody and blindfolded hanging from a tree.[272] Here, the child symbolically repeats the king's violence in an attempt to overcome her trauma. While the king murders different women for the crime of his wife's infidelity, the child diverts her violence on the witness as she is unable to reach the perpetrator. This suggests that the child tries to prove the abuse did not happen simply by killing the witness. Similarly, violence does not allow the child to control of her psychological well-being and therefore the child takes up the act of narration to assist with the process of healing. The child is made to see a psychologist, which is also meant to be Shahrazad's position in the tales, and the psychologist is 'fed up [with her] telling fairy tales' while she is expected to divulge her traumatic incident.[273] While this is a narrative twist of the tales, this also suggests that the child aims to repeat the fairy tales with an understanding that it is possible to re-imagine her trauma in a different context.

The novel specifically repeats the same statements in the case of the abuse to draw attention to its significance in the narrative. The child encounters a strange man in the coal shed and the author dives into her mind to show the conflict she has with the gaze. The stranger deceives the child with a counting game. When the man says 'one', the child needs to close her eyes; on 'two', the child is to open her eyes and until 'three' arrives, no one is to leave the coal shed.[274] After she

---

270 Shafak, *The Gaze*, pp. 221–2.

271 Ibid., pp. 227–8.

272 Ibid., p. 203.

273 Shafak, *The Gaze*, p. 219.

274 I recognise the fact that repetition may also reproduce the act of the abuse. The novel demonstrates that another child reciting 'one, two, three […]' reminds the narrator of the abuse and her own counting to three. However, her eating habits are also repeated as a response to this reminder. This act manifests very similarly to that of Shahrayar

opens her eyes, she realises that the number two is followed by number three: the abuse. Although it is put forward as a game by the harasser, this might also be a systematisation of the incident by the child. After the stranger ejaculates in the child's mouth, she initially vomits and then begins an attempt to purify her body from the influence of the stranger and her vomit. The novel relates the child's conflict and her attempts to cleanse it: '[s]he went to the bathroom. She washed out her mouth. She took off her dress. She washed out her mouth. She soaped the sponge. She washed out her mouth. She sponged herself. She washed out her mouth [...]'.[275] The child is represented as anxious to cleanse her mouth of the taste that has not left her mouth. Both the act of 'washing the mouth' and its narration are repeated incessantly. This process could be likened to Shahrazad using narrative and sexuality each night repetitively. The child aims to distance herself from the sexual abuse while Shahrazad aims to distance herself from being murdered. Washing her mouth is changed to eating compulsions soon afterwards: 'She was so hungry that [...] her hunger started eating at the deathly weight that was pressing down on her. But she still couldn't get rid of the terrible taste in her mouth. She urgently had to eat something else. [...] The more she ate the hungrier she got.'[276] Eating becomes a form of purifying the body from the effects of her violation. Although I recognise that repetition may also lead to reliving the abuse, here the child constructs a repetitive process of disrupting her own body (and body image), through which the experience of the abuse is also potentially disrupted. Therefore, she feels the need to eat more and more because she is distanced from the bitter taste, rather the bitter memory, left in her mouth and mind. Here, repetition of the eating act structures the identity of the narrator as an adult since she becomes fat and thus marginalised. Consequently, her body deviates from social norms of beauty. Therefore, I suggest that this act of repetition is a desire to alter the social norms that enabled the trauma in the first place. While it does not heal the child, it opens up the potential for her to re-imagine a new way of being without the abuse.

The novel imagines a re-embodiment of the child in a fat body to interrogate the social norms of beauty. The way the child cleans her mouth from the

---

and Shahrazad, in the way that Shahrazad responds to Shahrayar, who repeats the act of murdering women by perpetually repeating her tales. I would therefore suggest repetition is important in postcolonial feminine writing as a response to repeated gender and social norms. I discuss this in relation to haunting and postcolonialism in the Introduction on p. 27.

275 Shafak, *The Gaze*, p. 223.
276 Ibid., p. 224.

ejaculate also becomes the way she distances the memory from her mind. So, both her body and her mind are purified when eating is repeated, and the child eventually becomes fat. The child is reminded repeatedly 'if you continue to eat this way, you are going to become a very fat lady in the future. Then no one will like you. You know that, don't you? Do you want everyone to call you fatty?'.[277] The repeated act of eating becomes the child's act of resistance. She maintains over-eating 'with a hidden smile' because the child assumes that she can deflect the gaze on her by being fat and unlovable.[278] She relates her abuse to conforming to the social norms and being available for the harasser's gaze. Thus, the novel benefits from the repetition of the eating act to challenge social norms and the gaze. Shafak discusses in an interview that over-eating and fatness in the novel are deliberate acts to deform 'the form [the narrator] was encapsulated in, the body she has to take care of so that she can be "valuable as a woman"', because the narrator deems 'the subject of the Gaze' unchallengeable.[279] Therefore, fatness aims to deflect the male/authorial gaze from her body. However, it fails to deflect all the gazes on her because she feels 'the neighbour-ladies' eyes were always on us'.[280] Here, the neighbour-ladies' gazes creates an understanding of the female gaze that follows the patriarchal norms and is therefore still restrictive. B-C's gaze differs for the fat woman for the most part because he is non-normative himself and that makes her feel free of social boundaries. The narrator says,

> I could be free both of the body that enclosed me and of the kinds of looks that made me uncomfortable. [...] I gained the ability to see through my body and into myself [and] discovered new aspects of myself. [...] I was loveable when I looked into B-C's eyes. [...] Whatever I looked at through [his glasses], the lenses didn't solve the mystery [of how he saw it all].[281]

The passage suggests that the narrator aims to re-iterate B-C's 'loving' gaze by re-creating it with his glasses. She attempts to re-construct what he sees through his glasses when she tries them on and analyses herself and other objects. His glasses do not solve the mystery because his gaze is a part of him. However, his gaze is proven to be an illusion and not repeatable when the narrator discovers B-C calling her 'fatty' in his dictionary. This deconstructs the narrator's self-image through her lover's eyes and calls for a re-embodiment of the self.

---

277 Shafak, *The Gaze*, p. 223.
278 Ibid., p. 223.
279 Chancy, 'Migrations', p. 76.
280 Shafak, *The Gaze*, p. 241.
281 Ibid., p. 241.

The Gaze repeatedly uses a pattern of marginalised characters, which suggests an interrogation of the boundaries of embodiment. Similarly, characters in Shahrazad's storytelling usually have the same or similar names with different stories or different names within similar stories. *The Gaze* uses different characters with different names; however, they are repeated in a pattern. I would suggest that the novel questions the embodiment of these marginalised characters and re-imagines them in different trans-historical and transnational contexts, which allow for this interrogation. Therefore, the links between B-C and Keramet, and between the narrator, the Sable Girl and La Belle Annabelle are repeated and thus transcend temporal and spatial boundaries as well as narrative boundaries because these repetitions result in a re-definition of the characters in different bodies. I would suggest that the novel connects these characters regardless of time – centuries apart – and space – in different countries – and this disrupts the linearity of historical narration. It aims to decolonise narrative boundaries. Both B-C and Keramet have non-normative bodies and their bodies make them the focus of the normative gaze. The novel reveals similarities between Keramet and B-C as Keramet had 'two thin slits for' eyes that were drawn by his aunt and 'his eyes as always, were mute as ever'.[282] Similarly, 'B-C's eyes were reduced to two short, thin lines, and it was as if [...] they were closing. [H]is eyes didn't express anything and you couldn't put a finger on what he felt'.[283] However, what makes them almost doppelgangers is beyond their similarities in having non-normative bodies, which do not conform to social norms. Both characters work to return the gaze on society, and this would suggest that they aim to re-embody the gaze that constructs their identities. This gives both B-C and Keramet temporary authority over the gaze since they can control who looks at whom and how. These non-normative characters succeed in having powerful positions as the authority of the gaze because they control both subject and object positions of the gaze. B-C compiles a 'Dictionary of Gazes' that objectifies other people such as the fat narrator of the novel, and makes a spectacle of her for his gaze. With this dictionary, B-C offers his readers a compilation of stories about 'freaks', and this allows him to avoid the gaze turning on him. Similarly, Keramet establishes freak show tents for both male and female spectators. In these tents, Keramet provides the audience with an exhibit of non-normative characters. This enables him the power to manipulate positions of the gaze. More importantly, it allows him invisibility

---

282 Shafak, *The Gaze*, pp. 36–9.
283 Ibid., p. 80.

because there are other non-normative objects to be looked at. Thus, I would suggest that both characters hold a temporary position of authority.

The narrator is re-imagined as a character in both the Sable-Girl and La Belle Annabelle. The analysis of each character proves to have strong similarities in their formulation of identity despite their bodily differences. This suggests that the frustration of the narrator with the gaze is represented through the imaginary world with two distinct characters, as both characters are born as a result of the trauma caused by the gaze of the other. The narrator suffers sexual abuse as a child and this leads to her over-eating as a way of cleansing her body of the abuse and the gaze of her harasser. The narrator becomes fat and a victim of the gaze. This trauma that the gaze imposes is re-imagined with the Sable Girl and Annabelle. Naddaff argues:

> One cannot, however, posit repetition without simultaneously positing difference. No action, no matter how carefully imitated, can ever exactly repeat its precursor, for the very fact of its imitation, its repetition, necessitates its occurring at a different moment, and consequently, its having a different status. [...] The similarity perceived in dissimilars relies upon the relation of difference and distance as well as of resemblance and proximity between the two terms of the metaphor.[284]

Following Butler's exploration of gendered norms as repeated and Fanon's discussion of (un)veiling as a subversive repetition, here I would argue that the repetition of the same narrative with differences brings the potential for undoing narrative as well. The fact that the narrator is repeated in different times and spaces indicates that the gaze and trauma are narrated in a circular way and could be repeated to undo the very effects of trauma. While there are similarities in how the characters are created/born, they are quite different in terms of how they are embodied. I would argue that the repetition of the narrator in two different characters depends on differences more than similarities. Similarly, Annabelle's birth is supernatural as her mother imagines Annabelle's conception with the subject of a painting, which makes her supernaturally beautiful and still an object of the gaze. The narrator's sexual abuse as a child leads to her being overweight and she still cannot avoid being object of the gaze. Being fat creates a repetition of trauma which is caused by the gaze. Although the novel undermines the effects of trauma by repeatedly deforming the characters, it also suggests that repetition of the normative gaze is still restrictive.

The repetition of the characters with differences indicates how Shafak writes in the context of postcolonial feminine writing to transform boundaries of her

---

284 Naddaff, *Arabesque*, p. 54.

narrative while mimicking Shahrazad's storytelling. The novel offers a liberating space to explore these re-imagined characters when it shifts genre to fantasy. The Sable-Boy, who is the ancestor of Keramet's Sable-Girl, comes out of a shaman-istic ritual where the boy and the sable unite and begin a transformation. During the transformation, the ritual is interrupted by a sable hunter and the spell is broken. Therefore, 'they could neither step back and return to their former states, nor could they step forward and complete their transformation'.[285] The military governor exploits the hybrid boy and uses him to impregnate a sex-worker to create a sable-human hybrid ancestry: 'In every generation, those carrying the military governor's surname were the ones who displayed; those who inherited the Sable-Boy's condition were the displayed'.[286] The Sable-Boy and his lineage become a monstrous spectacle and are continuously exploited until the Sable-Girl is taken to Keramet's tent. Here, it becomes a way for the text to undermine the normative gaze on the Sable-Girl. The novel distinguishes between the Sable-Girl and her ancestor the Sable-Boy in terms of how they respond to patriar-chal authority. It would be expected that the Sable-Boy can always hold power over the gaze. However, the Sable-Boy conforms to societal norms and being a 'freak' spectacle. He strictly follows orders and therefore he is easily controlled by the governor, who exploits his non-normativity by forcing him to procreate. Contrarily, the novel demonstrates the Sable-Girl as a violent spectacle, whose anger prompts the audience to close their eyes. Although she is displayed as a horrifying object in the tent, I would suggest that this allows the Sable-Girl freedom to test her boundaries on stage. The Sable-Girl develops a sense of anger at the audience and she is not afraid to show it. Furthermore, I would argue that this anger is a form of voice recognised in postcolonial feminine writing. As the Sable-Girl is repeatedly exhibited on stage, she develops a voice of her own in her scream to both respond and resist. The fact that it does not register as a form of speech does not mean that she lacks a voice. On the contrary, she reclaims the power of the gaze when she uses her voice and forces the audience to close their eyes. It is a position very similar to Shahrazad, as she also must use her voice night after night for a temporary shift of power. Like Shahrazad, she reclaims her power over the gaze and actively resists the patriarchal authority even though it means she will stay within these boundaries indefinitely.

The stories of the Sable Girl and Annabelle are further explored toward the end of the novel and depict different endings that are not interrupted by the

---

285 Shafak, *The Gaze*, p. 59.
286 Shafak, *The Gaze*, p. 65.

external gaze. Shafak introduces the tale of the sable and the man who witnessed the transformation ritual: '[w]hen Timofei Ankidinov saw this enormous sable he was so surprised and so excited that he had difficulty keeping himself from crying out loud' and his gaze intervenes in the middle of the transformation.[287] Later Shafak returns to this beginning of the story:

> Timofei Ankidinov couldn't believe his eyes when he saw that huge sable go into the basket and disappear. [...] But suddenly, whatever it was that went through his mind, he took a step backward. He'd changed his mind. He wasn't going to open the basket, he wasn't going to look inside. [...] If Timofei Ankidinov had insisted on seeing what he shouldn't see, this sin would in the future result in the Sable-Girl being surrounded by people who wanted to see terrible ugliness. But because he didn't open the box, nothing like this happened.[288]

This indicates that neither the Sable-Girl nor Annabelle come into being if not gazed at. The novel's return to re-write the beginning of the sable's and similarly to Annabelle's stories negates the course of events, as Keramet checks his tents and '[t]he Sable-Girl [is not] there'.[289] Thus, the text narrates the same stories twice with different endings that would challenge the viability of each story. However, this repetition of the subsequent stories with a twist at the end provides the text with the possibility of challenging the gaze. If the ritual was not interrupted with an external gaze, the Sable-Girl would not come into being and it would be possible to question the gaze of the narrator. When the gaze is not penetrating, the story has a different outcome: 'the basket opened of its own accord. The beardless youth emerged having taken part of the sable's soul and having added a part of his soul to the sable's. He was now the tribe's shaman. [T]he name Sable-Girl never appeared'.[290] Shafak here writes a new story which she starts by merely repeating. However, repetition here creates a different form of body when it is not interrupted by the penetrating gaze of others. Here, the very absence of the gaze leads to a different being with the half-soul of the sable and the other half-soul of a human. A new form of being comes into existence without being objectified by the outside gaze. When the gaze is absent from this formation, 'the beardless youth' had the opportunity to define his own boundaries and he does not become a spectacle as the Sable-Girl would. With the act of repetition,

---

287 Shafak, *The Gaze*, p. 58.
288 Ibid., pp. 252–3.
289 Ibid., p. 253.
290 Ibid., p. 253.

Shafak is re-writing the same story to re-define the process of embodiment and the boundaries of the body.

Liberation of the Gaze and Voice of the Other

Building on the idea of repetition, this section explores how the characters in the novel use their bodies to interrogate their social boundaries and actively undermine the boundaries of the gaze. The novel uses the act of disguise to create a liberating space where the characters act out consensual roles. The novel shifts between the realms of fantasy and reality as the characters switch gender and social (class) roles. Repeating this act of switching roles generates a temporary shift in power dynamics. Here, I expand upon Fanon's discussion of the veil in a colonial context to explore the veil as a form of gender non-conforming disguise.

The narrator has a highly problematic connection to the gaze. She is depicted as extremely uncomfortable because she is the object of the gaze. However, it is clear that she also needs the gaze for her identity to be recognised. She talks about her experience in a bus and how she is seen as the source of inconvenience. The woman sitting next to her watches the fat woman 'out of the corner of her eye' and makes 'exaggerated movements to show that she's not going to be able to get comfortable, [...] and keeps huffing and puffing in complaint. I know this type well. I know why they behave the way they do. I'm used to it. These kinds of things happen to me all the time'.[291] Here, the fat woman is aware of her image and this image determines how she sees herself. She becomes more withdrawn and she tries 'not to make eye contact with any of the eyes that examine [her] with curiosity, and point [her] out to one another'.[292] However, she is curious of her image in the eyes of her dwarf partner and seeks to know how she is perceived by him because she assumes his gaze is loving. She describes her experience of searching for the gaze that somehow validates her identity:

> Whenever he fell asleep, and I took off the glasses that were sliding off the end of his nose, I would always try them on before I put them aside. What did his little eyes see through this glass? He knew so many amazing things, so much about people's stories, and how did he see it all? Whatever I looked at through them, the lenses of these glasses didn't solve the mystery. Whenever I put on B-C's glasses, I went to the mirror to look at myself. There would be nothing different about me; *my face was always the same face, my body the same body.*[293]

---

291 Shafak, *The Gaze*, pp. 20–1.
292 Ibid., p. 21.
293 Ibid., pp. 157–8, my emphasis.

With this act, she deliberately seeks the gaze. She wants, or rather, needs to have her identity recognised. As she has already internalised the other's gaze, she scrutinises her self-image with that gaze even when she attempts to put the layer of a lover's unthreatening gaze between herself and her image. Therefore, I would argue that the gaze she internalises is a learned act, rather than self-inflicted. When she looks at herself with B-C's glasses, her image does not change. What she sees in the mirror continues to be her image constructed in the gaze of others and therefore she is unable to reach the loving gaze. The narrator is disillusioned with her image especially because she still aims to construct her identity through B-C's gaze. Although the narrator does not see her image through B-C's eyes, she interrogates the possibility of multiple identities, which is further explored with different forms of disguises. This is a significant part of the novel because it allows the narrator to interrogate identity alongside her body image. The novel opens up the potential for creating alternatives to identity by exploring 'the false assumption that the Self is a monolithic – at least a consistent – whole'.[294] This act of re-creating self through others' eyes shows how the narrator's identity should not be considered 'monolithic'.

While she was reading through B-C's 'Dictionary of Gazes', she realises that B-C indeed sees her as research material. The way B-C relates the entry 'fatty' to the woman and his deliberate inquisition into her childhood create an anxiety in her identity because her feelings of safety with regards to her body, past trauma and the gaze are destroyed. It is the realisation that B-C objectifies her as fatty which makes her question the boundaries of her embodiment further. B-C describes her as '[s]he was so fat that wherever she went, people would stop whatever they were doing and stare at her. The way people looked at her made her so uncomfortable that she would eat even more and become even fatter'.[295] Therefore, she searches for ways to negotiate the borders of her shape:

> I was apprehensive about everything, but mostly about myself. […] I was unhappy. Like my stomach, my unhappiness grew the more it was fed. Of course it was possible to exist outside of these things; but I wasn't there. Now I am in the belly of hunger. […] I opened my mouth wide. I opened my mouth so wide that the hydrosphere was afraid I would drink up all the water and finish it. […] Neither water nor dirt could satisfy my hunger. I saw that it wouldn't work, so I decided to try air. I turned on the gas.[296]

---

294 Elif Shafak, 'Storytelling, Fake Worlds, and the Internet', *World Literature Today*, 89, 1 (2015), pp. 39–41, p. 41.

295 Shafak, *The Gaze*, p. 242.

296 Ibid., pp. 247–8.

This incident clearly causes a second trauma that pushes her into a relapse of over-eating. The stranger's abusive gaze here is likened to B-C's supposedly loving gaze. This section is narrated in a dream-like quality. The narrator is able to exceed her physical boundaries and consume food that would be inconsumable within human boundaries. By moving outside of the human's boundaries, the narrator refuses to be restricted to her physical shape. As the narrator creates a mouth/mind balance, her act demonstrates that she attempts to cleanse her mind through eating because her trauma is narrated as a hunger that encapsulates her. Since eating is indeed a response to her trauma, it becomes difficult to rule her mind with food. Thus, suicide arises as an option to overcome her physical and emotional boundaries of trauma and to shift her position as the subject of the gaze. Donna McCormack argues that 'bearing witness to trauma can take many creative forms, including cutting, burning and generally engaging the body in unexpected forms of communication'.[297] Here, the means of escaping the controlling gaze becomes the very means of destruction of the corporeal body. Transforming her human and gender boundaries allows the narrator to deal with the abuse and her disillusionment with B-C. Through her suicide, the narrator becomes a hot-air balloon and rises to the sky. The narrator's self is destroyed and re-embodied in a hot-air balloon disguise as a result of feeding her hunger, and thus it becomes difficult to define the narrator with a normative human body. Here, the novel deliberately uses the imagery of the hot-air balloon and disrupts the flow of the narrative in realistic time and space. Although postcolonial feminine writing does not guarantee a liberation from the restrictions of the gaze, as the balloon form can be seen in the sky by a child, it allows for the space to explore the narrator's own boundaries. It is therefore worth returning to Cixous's discussion of flight here as she proposes it as an empowering method for women alongside 'stealing' the patriarchal discourse. In this case, the narrator is not able to steal and transform the dominant gaze on her body. Therefore, she finds a 'hidden crossover' to her own embodiment, which allows her to transform both her corporeal form and her narrative. The narrator's body is intertwined with her narrative similar to that of Shahrazad's because she is able to blur the narrative by changing her corporeal form. Therefore, I would suggest that the act of flying gives the narrator and the narrative a form of fluidity and an ability to transgress the boundaries of reality and fantasy. It is through this 'flight' that the narrator

297 Donna McCormack, *Queer Postcolonial Narratives and the Ethics of Witnessing* (London and New York: Bloomsbury, 2014, 2015), p. 20.

gains the authority to control her own body and her own story as well as the forms through which her body communicates.

The novel suggests the creative use of disguise is subversive as it diverts the gaze. While the practice of (un)veiling allowed for Algerian women to cross colonial and gendered boundaries, the novel uses different props, a disguise, in order to create a liberating space. However, the success of disguise widely depends upon how these social and gender boundaries are re-worked. The narrator is irritated by the gaze she has endured all her life. In order to get rid of its effects, the narrator decides to change her appearance: 'So one day I decided to dye my hair. It was clear that I couldn't get rid of the letters f-a-t-t-y. but with the right hair colour I could make them invisible; like a sweater that doesn't show stains'.[298] This indicates that the narrator aims to create a sphere where she does not stand out by playing with body parts and trying to conform to a normative body. Although dyeing her hair does not earn her acceptance, she hopes to conform to the social norms with the right colour choice. However, this does not help her avoid the gaze and thus B-C convinces her to don a disguise to go out together, which would be even trickier for the narrator since she was aware 'We didn't please anyone's eyes. Even if we were in disguise, and even at night, we didn't suit each other'.[299] This suggests that the narrator in fact contradicts her acts with her expressions. While she attempts different forms of disguise, she does not believe it would be effective to subvert the gaze in an environment where social recognition is important for her identity. The narrator's effort to conform to society unfolds as not inherently successful because she reproduces social and gender norms rather than subverting them. I would therefore suggest that this form of disguise fails her once again because it does not question the ways in which her body is embodied.

Creative use of disguise on two separate occasions gives the narrator a sense of security, which her identity does not provide, as well as an ability to exceed gender roles and social boundaries. Her identity as a fat woman is not acceptable in society as she is always being pointed at by others. She considers supermarkets as 'the only place outside where I'm not judged for my fatness'.[300] Her identity is notable in a supermarket setting because '[a]t supermarkets I felt I was being given special treatment. [...] my obesity and gluttony were valid. And in the supermarkets their validity was accepted'.[301] However, she needs to change her

---

298 Shafak, *The Gaze*, p. 95.
299 Ibid., p. 99.
300 Shafak, *The Gaze*, p. 85.
301 Ibid., p. 86.

identity to be more validated and liberated elsewhere. Although the narrator's initial disguise with hair dye fails, the disguise of the narrator and B-C is effective because they do not conform to the roles they are given. The first time they go out in disguise, they switch gender roles. The narrator pretends to be a man: 'I sprinkled lots of hair all over myself. My hands, chest and legs were covered with hair. [...] My moustache wasn't so thick, but it would pass. Besides, there was no need for a beard. I'd become a coarse young man. I raised my eyebrows to tell B-C to walk in front of me'.[302] It is clear that when she is in disguise, she feels more comfortable with her identity. Here, the shift in gender roles undermines the gaze and gives the narrator a sense of authority over the gaze. She embraces masculinity and she follows the social, patriarchal codes by being a 'coarse young man' and leading B-C as if he is a submissive woman. While she embraces this new identity, it is strengthened when they are subjected to the gaze. The narrator is challenged by another man to 'leave the lady alone, man'.[303] This verbal attack immediately progresses into a fight which is fuelled by spectators. Therefore, her identity is validated as a man by a group of spectators who accept the narrator as a man. Furthermore, B-C reinforces the narrator's identity by being grateful: 'I looked at B-C, and saw that his tears had made tracks [...] on his cheeks. In front of everyone, his eyes shone with pleasure at my having fought for him'.[304] This representation of a fight for a lady is a subversion of expected gender roles. By performing masculine behaviour, the narrator is able to pass as a man and fulfil his masculine role as 'protector'. While the scene that they act out seems normative following the patriarchal order, the gaze indeed fails to recognise their embodied gender identities. Similar to Fanon, who discusses that Algerian women who took and left the veil as a form of anti-colonial disguise, the characters undermine the gaze by transgressing normative boundaries of gender through their bodies. They play out a fantasy that is recognised as normative. This suggests a shift of power dynamics, even temporarily. The characters undermine the gaze by playing with their gender roles wherein they are assumed to follow the traditional social order, and this makes their act powerful.

B-C is also able to get beyond the boundaries of gender and he fully embraces his new role as a woman. When he is dressed as a woman, he performs a feminine role as well. The narrator is shocked to observe: 'He passed coquettishly in front of me. I watched him with alarm. It struck me with terror to see the man

---

302 Ibid., pp. 100–1.
303 Ibid., p. 102.
304 Shafak, *The Gaze*, p. 103.

I love display an attitude I'd never seen him display before, and behave in a way that seemed not to acknowledge the past, make a lie of the present and to exclude me. [...] As if his personality changed with his appearance'.[305] With his appearance changed, B-C also undergoes a change of personality. He adopts a feminine identity and successfully performs it. The new identity almost liberates him from the past and the present. By creating a space where she dresses her body and mind as a woman, B-C creates a liberating space which undermines gendered norms. Marks suggests that it is possible to create a fully consensual environment which allows for dominant and submissive roles to be developed as fluid and enabling. Here, B-C constructs a liberating space to play a fantasy relationship with the narrator by temporarily switching his gender role. B-C develops an understanding for the feminine identity and his voice as a woman is just as powerful. He refuses to be compartmentalised in a fixed identity. Therefore, when he changes appearance, he is able to change his identity for a limited time and space. He rejoices in being watched when he makes a speech about being a woman:

> Within the four walls of home you want us to be playful and flirtatious, even whorish, but as soon as we step outside you want us to be demure and proper little ladies. You have no idea that when you're playing with our appearance you're playing with our pride. Aren't you men? You're all the same. If we went out and did a tenth of what you want us to do at home, you'd cry for blood immediately. Am I lying? Enough! I object to the splitting of my personality.[306]

While his voice is liberated in the case of being a woman, it is a fantasy played out in a limited time and space. His identity as a woman is a 'splitting of his personality'; however, it also subverts the clear-cut distinction between the past and the present. B-C purposefully defies his embodied gender identity as he complains about the patriarchal norms that women are confined to. He demonstrates a liberated voice, and this is also because he is being seen and recognised in performing his fantasy role. Nonetheless, he always reverts back to what he sees as his true gender role. Despite the fact that the fantasy role is fluid and enabling, it is limited to a consensual space and time.

Spectatorship in the novel aims to challenge the traditional gaze and create an opportunity for the narrator to be an active spectator. As an individual who has been subject to the violent effects of the gaze, the narrator is also frequently given the chance to look at others in the novel. She initially feels more comfortable watching B-C while he is sleeping and modelling: '[w]hen B-C was asleep in

---

305 Ibid., pp. 98–9.
306 Shafak, *The Gaze*, p. 105.

front of the television, I would take the opportunity to watch him. I would watch the hands that were too big to belong to a dwarf, the toes that all looked as if they belonged to different feet'.[307] Although B-C is sleeping as the narrator is closely watching him, he would be an easy spectacle for the narrator to directly gaze upon. As he is exposed to being the object of the gaze daily, he is represented as Other like herself in the novel. She aims to deconstruct his identity by closely analysing his body and face and deciding how he looks as if his features are randomly brought together. The second time they are disguised, they become a 'hardened cold-blooded thief [and his] sidekick; an unemployed shiftless adolescent'.[308] They aim to watch others eating in a restaurant while being unrecognisable: '[f]rom where we stood we could see that the mouthful the woman had been chewing daintily somehow wouldn't go down her throat. She was right to be uneasy. It must have been unpleasant to eat with us watching'.[309] Here, both are interrogating the boundaries of the gaze by challenging the people in the restaurant to eat while being stared at. This is a direct reference to how the narrator feels uncomfortable being looked at. However, the novel gives her the opportunity to look and return the gaze to others. The woman and her 'wrapped from head to toe in orange' family are attacked by 'cold-blooded thieves' after they leave the restaurant.[310] The text here depicts the family as not only dressed in the colour orange, but as an orange family. The narrator 'strip[s] off the orange peels the woman was wearing [with a knife], without injuring her at all' and challenges her husband to look at his wife and see her peeled.[311] While the boundary of fantasy and reality shifts, so do the power dynamics. While playing with fantastic forms in realistic environments, the novel offers the opportunity to re-define social and gender norms in a creative style and language. The novel re-embodies the characters in a way that they become meaningful subjects of the gaze. By blurring the distinction between fantasy and reality, Shafak takes over the narrative form and re-defines it by creating a tension between the gaze and the body.

B-C is also recognised as powerful when he poses as a model for the art students. He challenges others to openly look at his body and paint it. Changing the context of the stare-able object, freak shows have demonstrated that not only non-normative bodies are able to look/gaze back and not be vulnerable, but also

---

307 Shafak, *The Gaze*, pp. 157–8.
308 Ibid., p. 164.
309 Ibid., p. 166.
310 Ibid., p. 167.
311 Ibid., p. 168.

they subvert the gaze by benefiting from it. Rosemarie Garland-Thomson studies
the history of the 'freak' and suggests that the visualisation of 'freak' bodies is an
historical phenomenon, which once indicated 'divine wrath'.[312] The idea of seeing
freaks as spectacles develops when scientific inquiry begins to analyse, expose
and violate these bodies by displaying them at medical theatres. At the same time,
as Garland-Thomson relates, the institutionalised circuses politicise the essence
of the freak body by displaying them as a source of amusement and fascination
and also work to 'underpin sociopolitical subordination by representing difference as deviance'.[313] Here, B-C's freak body is displayed as a form of deviance
for spectators; however, his own positionality in this demonstration is usually
undermined. It is whether B-C or other marginalised figures want to be spectacles or not that changes their position when they are on display because it opens
up a possibility for them to gain agency by being seen. Garland-Thomson refers
to Lomnicki, 'a little woman who has made a career of her paradoxical appearance [who] earns her living by offering entertaining performances and her own
unusual body up for contemplation'.[314] Lomnicki says that '[o]n stage [...] my
disability works for me [...] being so different looking, people really take notice
[and] really get it'.[315] Lomnicki clearly wants to be looked at, to be seen. It gives
her and different others a possibility to be seen as who they are: 'everyday people
who go to work, drive cars and have kids – not just someone in a Mickey Mouse
costume'.[316] Therefore, I would suggest being on display also means being real
for B-C. By 'real', I mean the possibility of being ordinary and familiar. B-C is no
longer an essential spectacle and an unfamiliar freak but is instead recognised as
a human being. Garland-Thomson argues that being shut away through segregation and distancing 'thwarts opportunities for this recognition. To be recog-
nized, one needs literally to be seen'.[317] This contests the social order of looking
for B-C as well because the narrator thinks '[d]warves don't watch passers-by
in the street, or go shopping at supermarkets, or wander around in public. [...]

312 Rosemarie Garland-Thomson, *Freakery: Cultural Spectacles of the Extraordinary Body* (New York and London: New York UP, 1996), p. 1.
313 Ibid., p. 13.
314 Rosemarie Garland-Thomson, *Staring: How We Look* (Oxford: Oxford UP, 2009), p. 174.
315 Tekki Lomnicki, and Laurie Benz, 'Little Amazons in the Arts', 2000–04 <http://www.geocities.com/ltl_renaissance_feminist/Artful-Amazons1.html>, qtd in Garland-Thomson, *Staring*, p. 174. [I could not access this source].
316 Lomnicki and Benz, qtd in Garland-Thomson, *Staring*, p. 174.
317 Garland-Thomson, *Staring*, p. 194.

Dwarves are trapped in a state of invisibility; just like many people who are put on display. They don't want other people's eyes to see them'.[318] However, B-C behaves just the opposite of how a dwarf is expected to behave. He contests the idea that he is in a 'state of invisibility' by seeking the gaze directed at him. Moreover, he seeks ways to gaze at others.

B-C opens himself up to being scrutinised by others in order to gain recognition and to have a validated identity. He becomes more than an imaginary character who is out of the ordinary when he puts himself forward and challenges the others to describe him. The narrator reveals that none of the students could situate him in a fixed identity: 'But I think it was the strangeness of his eyes rather than the ephemeral nature of his stance that made the students' work difficult. [...] When B-C's eyes were closed none of the students' drawings resembles any of the others. [...] He just looked around with an aimless stare'.[319] Specifically because he seeks ways to display his body and to be looked at, B-C is challenging the dominant gaze on his body because it is liberating, rather than victimising him. Here, the deliberate intention in displaying his body as a response to the gaze upon him echoes Shahrazad's deliberate intention in marrying the king. Shahrazad offers her body to the king and reclaims the power of storytelling in return. Similarly, B-C offers his body to be seen and reclaims the power to his body by controlling the gaze upon him. Although he is in a vulnerable position with regards to the art students (his audience), he is still in a powerful position as he only allows his audience a limited space. He makes it impossible for the art students to capture his body in a still image by 'the strangeness of his eyes'. Furthermore, the fact that he is re-imagined on each canvas differently demonstrates how his identity could be recognised as unstable and difficult to situate. Therefore, this act also creates a liberating space for B-C where the power dynamics between B-C and the students shift. B-C gains authority over how people see and define him in the art studio where he is a voluntary spectacle. He encourages the narrator to display herself 'since [she] was already fat enough to attract the attention of anyone who saw [her], and since [she] was already being watched, then [she] should go and display [herself] out of spite'.[320] This indicates that B-C's modelling is an act of resistance to the gaze. Putting himself out to be analysed and encouraging the narrator to do so as she is already a spectacle; B-C intends to unsettle the norms of the dominant gaze.

---

318 Shafak, *The Gaze*, p. 233.
319 Ibid., p. 80.
320 Shafak, *The Gaze*, p. 81.

The novel subverts the male gaze and creates a pseudo-liberating space for women to gaze. Although this suggests a liberation of the female gaze, here, the female gaze follows the dominant codes of the male gaze. Therefore, it does not result in a fully liberated space. Keramet presents groups of othered bodies to thousands of women from different nations, ages and classes: '[h]e was aware that women were deeply pleased to see women uglier than themselves. He was going to show them what they wanted to see. In the cherry-coloured tent he wasn't going to display ugly women, or the ugliest women, but ugliness itself'.[321] Keramet gives an equal chance for women and men in separate tents to create their own accounts of looking. Here, women are able to construct a gaze of their own within a certain setting where they could negotiate their position of gazing. The spectacle of ugliness correlates to the image of woman in the male gaze. It is expected to give pleasure to the female spectators as it is assumed that they would like to see ugliness, as well as creating anxiety because it creates a proximity between themselves and the object of their desires. This anxiety is displayed when the snake charmer showed '[t]he world was reflected in reverse in the snake's eyes. In the world shown in the mirror of its eyes, virgins were widows and masters were slaves. [...] It was a description of hell [...] within life's bosom'.[322] Although women, who were not part of the normative male gaze, could freely look at the eyes of the object of their gazes, the object was not pleasing to look at and in turn it created fear of looking. So, they were reminded to 'close your eyes!' by '[a]n ear-splitting voice'.[323] This indicates a reversal of the male gaze, but it also reveals that the social position of gaze is negotiable; therefore, it is dynamic and changing. This circus-like act is repeated night after night with a similar result. Even though this position of acting a consensual scene is a temporary intervention in the dominant gaze, it is this temporary undermining of it every night that opens up the potential for transformation. The possibility of a liberating space, which permits the act of consensual roles, is therefore largely dependent on creating non-conforming gender and social roles, albeit in a temporary capacity.

Conclusion

This chapter has argued that *The Gaze* follows a pattern of narrative style that I name postcolonial feminine writing. The novel constructs and deconstructs

---

321 Shafak, *The Gaze*, p. 45.
322 Ibid., pp. 70–1.
323 Ibid., p. 74.

identity through the theme of the gaze. Although the novel resembles *1001 Nights* in both form and content, it also shows some differences considering Shafak wrote negations of the stories within the novel, and I captured how each story could be re-narrated in imaginative ways. The novel challenges the position of the dominant gaze by presenting the gaze in negotiable positions. The text consists of multiple gazes as well as multiple narrative layers, challenging dominant positions of gazing. I re-formulate the concept of the gaze as multiple and relational within the theoretical framework of postcolonial feminine writing.

Repetition becomes key to postcolonial feminine writing and as a literary device in the novel. Following Shahrazad's narrative style of the constant repetition of form and content, *The Gaze* uses the device of repetition to deconstruct gender and narrative and explores time and space as non-linear and transforming. Apart from narrative voice, both form and content including multiple characters are constantly repeated. Repetition results in a different outcome when the gaze is re-imagined in a new and different context.

The previous section has argued that the concept of the gaze enables various marginalised characters to test their own boundaries and re-imagine their identities. The novel employs the creative use of disguise to re-define the identities of these characters. More specifically, the text creates liberating spaces, which allow the characters to re-define their social and gender boundaries. Moreover, disguise opens up the potential for the characters to generate their own gazes and to reflect the gaze back to the so-called subjects of the gaze. Therefore, *The Gaze* provides different and multiple positions of looking and gives the opportunity for the non-normative characters to re-imagine different positions of looking.

While this potential for liberating spaces is sought through the fat and dwarf bodies in *The Gaze*, concentrating on Shafak's *Honour* (2012), my third chapter will take a different turn by focusing on how bodies become forms of expression if the voice is dominated by patriarchal systems of power. This indeed develops how postcolonial feminine writing re-imagines different liberating spaces that enable other women to access narrative voice.

Chapter III: Silences and Shames in Shafak's *Honour* (2012)

Introduction

This chapter explores how Shafak re-creates Shahrazadean storytelling in a diasporic context in the novel, *Honour* (2012).[324] I will focus on how Shafak re-conceptualises the forms of silence, speech, honour and shame in order to liberate female characters from patriarchal and narrative boundaries. The narrator of the novel replicates Shahrazad's position of storytelling and in doing so creates a cycle of narratives that challenges the patriarchal order through multiple narrative voices. By questioning and blurring the distinction between 'mother, virgin and prostitute', I suggest that the novel liberates women's sexuality from the pre-designated restrictions of shame.[325] In particular, I argue that silence offers the potential to recognise women's existences by refusing to replicate the patriarchal language and therefore becomes a form of resistance. Indeed, Shafak unsettles dominant interpretations of silence and voice by exploring how these concepts relate to the reproduction of power dynamics. Such narrative innovations convey that women need to use caution when it comes to voice. That is, even though speech is often equated with liberation, this novel shows how voice may simply serve to reproduce the patriarchal order. By playing with the binary oppositions of speech and silence, honour and shame, *Honour* undermines the very idea that these are opposing notions. Instead, I argue that Shafak shows how silence may be a postcolonial feminine technique that facilitates access to a powerful position that is neither patriarchal nor simply submissive, but in many ways what I am calling liberating. Indeed, I want to suggest that bodies and senses can substitute voice when this voice conforms to patriarchal power structures.[326] To this extent, Shafak's

---

324 This novel is first published by Viking in 2012. I will be referring to the 2013 Penguin edition. Elif Shafak, *Honour* (London and New York: Penguin, 2013).

325 Here, I borrow the social categories of women as 'mothers, virgins and prostitutes' from Luce Irigaray's 'Women on the Market' in *This Sex Which is not One*.

326 I focus specifically on how the senses of smell and sight are re-formulated as forms of communication for *Honour*'s Jamila in this chapter. See also Claire Chambers's *Making Sense of British Muslim Novels* for an extensive analysis of senses (touch, sound, sight and smell) in postcolonial narratives.

narrative structure, themes and non-binary positionalities are part of the technique that I define as postcolonial feminine writing. Here, this is defined as Shahrazad's mode of storytelling, which is simultaneously a site of postcolonial resistance that is specifically feminine, refusing structural and thematic boundaries of the patriarchal narratives and offering an alternative to dominant narrative discourse.

Honour focuses largely on an immigrant multi-ethnic family and deals with the clash of honour and shame within this familial and diasporic context. Following Shahrazadean storytelling in both structure and themes, *Honour* shows a striking resemblance to Shafak's *The Gaze* (2006) and al-Shaykh's *1001 Nights*. While *The Gaze* focuses on the potential of liberation and agency through deconstructing and re-constructing the gaze, *Honour* focuses on deconstructing patriarchal norms of femininity and masculinity through the binary of honour and shame, and silence and voice. Similar to the Shahrazadean tradition of narrative in *The Gaze*, the narrative form in *Honour* is not linear, but disrupted frequently with diary entries and letters. The novel is set in multiple times and spaces, and uses multiple narrative voices; it is also written in a circular form like *The Gaze*. I would suggest that the novel reflects on this transformation of time and space by re-naming the male protagonist, Askander/Iskender/Alexander. Similar to how al-Shaykh re-creates genitalia as multiple by re-naming them, Shafak re-creates this character in each historical and national context. I would therefore suggest that *Honour* re-imagines fluidity and multiplicity of identity through this character like al-Shaykh's *Nights*. Alex's family is of Kurdish and Turkish origins. Alex is born in a Kurdish-dwelling village in eastern Turkey and initially named Askander. Upon the family's migration to Istanbul, he is re-named Iskender, and subsequently re-named Alexander when they migrate to London. The evolution of Alex's name also transforms how he experiences social and gender norms differently when he migrates. This is evident when Alex employs patriarchal social and gender norms for his family, even in London, he disregards these norms for his English girlfriend, Katie. Moreover, I would suggest that *Honour* shows a similar interpretation of the concepts of honour and shame to that of the gaze in *The Gaze*, which as we have seen is a changeable, re-constructible positions of looking defined in a consensual environment. The narrative present time in the novel is frequently interrupted with flashbacks and foreshadowing.

Honour begins and finishes with the release of one of the main characters Iskender/Alex from prison where he served a sentence because he murdered his mother's twin sister, Jamila, whom Alex confused with his mother, Pembe. Esma, Alex's sister, begins narrating accounts of their parents' earlier lives before

Alex's release from prison as she promised herself that she would not let her mother's story be forgotten. Therefore, Esma aims to 'send it into some corner of the universe where it could float freely, away from [them]'.[327] Esma gives voice to the silenced memories and past traumas, which otherwise would not be heard. Petya Tsoneva Ivanova argues that this ensures Esma's narrative confession will lead the way for 'other silenced stories of oppression'.[328] I would therefore suggest Esma becomes the storyteller of stories that would be transferred orally or in written form from generation to generation, similar to Shahrazad giving voice to other silences.[329] Furthermore, these accounts disrupt the linearity of the narrative. Here, Esma creates a cycle of narratives which are repeated in non-linear time. The present time of the narrative is inevitably haunted by the past and the future. Thus, the storyteller's role is to blend the present, the past and the future in order to recognise silent or silenced narratives. This is a significant aspect of the novel because it contributes to the understanding of a never-ending narrative structure. While dominant narrative structures impose linearity that almost always excludes femininity, this type of storytelling suggests an uncontrollable and subversive feminine desire through writing.

Although Esma is acknowledged as the principal narrator who aims to have the story of their mother acknowledged and heard by other people, Alex's diary entries from prison interrupt the main narrative. His version of the narrative offers a different perspective from Esma's narration. Thus, *Honour* has a similar cycle of narration to *The Gaze* by narrating and undoing the same story; in other words, each story is told differently by each narrator: Esma and Alex. While Esma narrates her ideas and her life in the present (set in 1992) in the first-person, the accounts around her parents' lives are narrated in the third-person. The sections which are narrated in the third-person are titled with relevant objects or the focus of the section, while the first-person narration is always clearly Esma's voice. All chapters begin with the time and place of the narrative, which blurs the lines between reality and fiction. Historicising the events to a specific setting conveys that they are real. However, from the beginning it is

---

327 Shafak, *Honour*, p. 1.

328 Petya Tsoneva Ivanova, *Negotiating Borderlines in Four Contemporary Migrant Writers from the Middle East* (Newcastle upon Tyne: Cambridge Scholars Publishing, 2018), p. 192.

329 The novel re-creates the story of twin sisters, Pembe and Jamila, in the next generation as Esma's twin daughters, Layla and Jamila. While the text repeats the motif of twins, it also enables Esma to re-imagine her mother's story through her daughters, as she raises her daughters more independently.

clarified that Esma wants to make her mother's story heard, which she has only learnt by reading her letters and not witnessed personally. Alex's diary entries always follow accounts of Esma's narration of their family life with her siblings and offer Alex's perspective of his time in prison. These entries start with how Alex discovers his mother's affair upon finding her dishevelled at home and he can almost '*touch her guilt* [and] *smell her shame*' in her movements.[330] Therefore, he decides to buy a knife only to '*scare*' her or her lover and not to hurt anybody physically.[331] Through Alex's version of events, Shafak demonstrates that Alex is manipulated by different patriarchal figures in his life such as his uncle Tariq and a group leader (against racist attacks on immigrants), who argues against feminism as 'a Western thing'.[332] Here, the novel contextualises violence, revealing how patriarchal and racial structures also restrict masculinity to violent expression towards women.

The novel's portrayal of masculinity indicates an intimacy with patriarchy. The novel is titled *Iskender*, 'Alexander', and Shafak cross-dresses as Alex on the cover of the novel. In an interview with *The Guardian*, Shafak says that she usually hides in her male characters rather than identifying with any of her female characters.[333] This shows how the novel is situated in relation to masculinity and patriarchal norms. It pays close attention to the portrayal of male characters to show how masculinity is manifested in society. The control patriarchy holds over male characters is just as restrictive as that over women. Likewise, Nuzhat Khan suggests that this indicates an active role of women in the patriarchal construction of masculinity in society as Alex is encouraged to be patriarchal and dominant by his mother.[334] Although *Honour* clarifies that Alex is guilty of murder, an honour-killing, the novel implies that Alex is raised to maintain patriarchal norms by his family, including his mother, and therefore he is not solely to blame. This is further explored through his time in prison where he realises his wrongdoing and writes letters to his mother to ask for her forgiveness. The novel

---

330 Shafak, *Honour*, p. 51. Alex's prison diary is italicised and differentiated from the main narrative in the text.

331 Ibid., p. 51, emphasis in original.

332 Shafak, *Honour*, p. 216.

333 Kate Kellaway, 'Interview: Elif Shafak', *The Guardian*, 5th Feb 2017, <https://www.theguardian.com/books/2017/feb/05/elif-shafak-turkey-three-daughters-of-eve-interview>[accessed 15th Jan 2019].

334 Nuzhat Khan, 'Accountability in Honour Killings: Reading of Elif Shafak's *Honour*', *PARIPEX – Indian Journal of Research*, 6, 6 (2017), pp. 477–80, p. 477.

indicates that the potential for women's liberation from patriarchy also requires the liberation of masculinity from patriarchal constraints.

The novel focuses on ideals of family honour which is based on the social and patriarchal control of women's sexuality and desires. While the novel mainly focuses on the murder of Jamila (twin sister) mistaken for Pembe (mother) by Alex with the reinforcement of his uncle Tariq, there are other accounts of family honour issues in the novel that result in abandonment and/or death. Pembe and Jamila witness that their older sister Hediye is forced by her family to commit suicide as their father is reluctant to kill her even though he was expected by society to cleanse his family's honour. Similarly, Jamila is abandoned by Adem upon his discovery of Jamila's questionable virginity. Adem's own mother is also described as a source of shame for their family because she elopes with her lover. However, the narrative also underlines how Adem's mother was terribly vulnerable to her husband who frequently committed physical abuse against her and their children. Uncle Tariq, who has become responsible for his family honour and has suffered public shame due to his mother's actions, is therefore excessively offended by his sister-in-law's affair.

The text is therefore structured to reflect a dichotomy of honour and shame. This binary opposition is a critique of the traditional construction of feminine and masculine roles. The norm of honour has almost always been associated with men and therefore has effectively limited women's access to it. The text criticises forms of honour and shame in order to reveal how these norms are socially-constructed and open to interpretation. Both honour and shame are usually considered Eastern concepts that indicate inferiority of the East for the West. These concepts suggest the restriction of women through the control of female sexuality 'whereby honour is seen as the attribute of men and shame of women'.[335] However, honour and shame should not and cannot simply be reduced to Eastern concepts. Bahar Davary argues that shame and honour are universal norms that are different across time periods and cultures, 'yet similar in that they shape aspects of one's identity'.[336] While the norm of shame mostly relates to sexuality for women, it is related to social respect and the protection of family honour, which is predominantly defined through the control of women's

---

335 Aylin Akpinar, 'The Honour/Shame Complex Revisited: Violence against Women in the Migration Context', *Women's Studies International Forum*, 26, 5 (2003), pp.425–42, p. 430.

336 Bahar Davary, 'Miss Elsa and the Veil: Honor, Shame, and Identity Negotiations', *Journal of Feminist Studies in Religion*, 25, 2 (2009), pp. 47–66, p. 48.

behaviour, for men. Thus, concepts of shame and honour shape women's private and public roles. Having introduced the novel, I want to explore how shame manifests in the patriarchal order and the potentials of re-formulating shame.

Shame is a feeling that is 'felt by and on the body'.[337] Sara Ahmed argues that shame is an emotion that is reproduced through heteronormativity when one fails to approximate a social ideal.[338] Shame constructs a boundary between people who feel shame and those who witness their shame. While social norms are reproduced with a social 'contract', 'the success or failure of subjects' to maintain this social ideal causes the person to develop feelings of shame or pride.[339] While this is usually discussed with respect to female sexuality in an Eastern context, Ahmed highlights that any non-normative act such as 'queer desires, which depart from the "form" of the loving nuclear family [and] become an injury [...] to the bodily form of the social norm' may form feelings of shame. Therefore, shame in this context works to reproduce patriarchal and heteronormative norms and ideals that aim to restrict minorities' and women's identities. As the body demonstrates feelings of shame, the skin is also 'impressed' with 'the physicality of shame'.[340] The body shows clear images of being shamed or feeling shamed through 'head hung, downcast or averted eyes, changing in skin tone, lowered voice or silenced speech, frozen facial expressions, slouched posture'.[341] The body is vulnerable to feelings of shame, and how shame is felt 'on and through bodies [...] means that shame also involves de-forming and re-forming of bodily and social spaces, as bodies "turn away" from the others who witness the shame'.[342] Shame creates boundaries by forming a division between people who experience shame and their witnesses. This suggests shame is a significant norm in shaping and enforcing heteronormativity on 'bodily spaces'.

Shame theorist Gershen Kaufman discusses that shame is a 'multidimensional [and] multi-layered experience' as it is both an individual phenomenon and also a collective ideal that is 'reproduced within families, and each culture

---

337 Sara Ahmed, *The Cultural Politics of Emotion* (Edinburgh: Edinburgh UP, 2004), p. 103.

338 Ibid., p. 107.

339 Ibid., p. 109. Ahmed discusses how collective ideals work to reproduce national pride or shame in a postcolonial Australian context.

340 Ibid., p. 103.

341 Robert G. Lee, and Gordon Wheeler, *The Voice of Shame: Silence and Connection in Psychotherapy* (Cambridge, MA: Gestalt Press, 1996, 2003), p. 6.

342 Ahmed, *The Cultural Politics of Emotion*, p. 103.

has its own distinct sources as well as targets of shame'.[343] Therefore, concepts of honour and shame retain both private and public aspects. While it is practised by and on the body on an individual level, the practice of shame as a collective norm forces people into feeling shame even when they do not feel shame privately. Similarly, honour has both public and private faces. James Brandon and Salam Hafez conducted a study on honour-based violence in the UK and argue that 'in all societies honour has both a private and public aspect. [Honour becomes an] individual's self-respect'; how a person sees himself and his relative value in society. But at the same time, measures of honour also dictate the extent to which society accept a person's self-worth'.[344] While honour is felt by the body as someone's self-worth, it is also significant in how a person is recognised by the society. This public aspect of honour is usually marked through how women's sexuality is controlled in the private sphere. Women's bodies are significant 'objects' that retain both public and private boundaries within themselves. The concepts of honour and shame are the means through which women are constrained as 'private property' by the patriarchal order. Honour and shame are constructed as binary opposites and in turn they may separate the self/private as distinct from the other/public.

The female body is socially constructed as shameful in Eastern societies as well. Nawal El Saadawi focuses on how shame manifests in Arab societies and states that there is a distorted sense of honour in effect. A man's honour is regarded with the segregation of sexes and the subordination of female members of the family who have to 'keep their hymens intact. [...] He can be a womanizer of the worst calibre and yet be considered an honourable man as long as his womenfolk are able to protect their genital organs'.[345] El Saadawi concentrates on how moral norms are manifested differently for women and men in society. While sexual purity for female members of the society remains as the most significant aspect of a man's honour, male sexuality is not defined by shame.[346] Whereas men are

---

343 Gershen Kaufman, *Shame: The Power of Caring* (Cambridge, MA: Schenkman, 1980), p. 191.
344 James Brandon and Salam Hafez, *Crimes of the Community: Honour-based Violence in the UK* (London: Centre for Social Cohesion CIVITAS, 2008), p. 3. This study is predominantly about honour crimes in immigrant communities in the UK.
345 Nawal El Saadawi, *The Hidden Face of Eve* (London: Zed Books, 1980, 2007, 2015), p. 64.
346 Here, El Saadawi focuses her argument on heteronormative male sexuality and I retain the 'male sexuality' in a heteronormative sense, as well. I do not concentrate on how queer identities would posit different relations to the norms of shame and honour.

not shamed if they embrace their sexuality, it becomes a source of social deg-
radation for the family and society on the account of female sexual experience.
Along the lines of El Saadawi, Beth Baron discusses that honour is a collective affair that helps the reproduction of the parameters of the collective norms. Baron
argues that the honour of an entire family 'resides in the conduct of its women'.[347]
Both Baron and El Saadawi emphasise that honour and shame construct female
sexuality at the border of the public and private spheres, and as determining
a sense of belonging. As honour and shame result from the individual and/or
communal performances of a 'shameful' act, they can also be undermined by the
performance of this act. I would therefore suggest that these terms should be re-
imagined in order to reflect the complexity: shame is not simply defined by (the
lack of) honour, and shamelessness is the possibility to recognise and undermine
the norm of shame.

The concepts of shame and honour are specifically reproduced to maintain
the identity of the self and the other in this novel. The text contextualises family
honour and shame as a part of immigrant experience. Although the context does
not suggest exile, but a migration for economic reasons, the focus of the text
gives recognition to the experiences of a small immigrant community that is
bound by gender, class and ethnic norms. These ideas become more compel-
ling within a diasporic community because they define a sense of belonging that
preserves communal unity. Namrata Mitra discusses that the sexual purity of
women is also important on a communal and national level and that a sexual
taint indicates a loss of national honour.[348] Mitra argues that 'an attack against
women's sexual organs is marked by a desire to annihilate the other community,
not only through massacres, but also by mutilating and tattooing sexual organs
that could have actually borne subsequent generations'.[349] Here, the protection of
national honour depends on the protection of the women of the nation against
the other community. Women's sexualities are embodied as the future of the nation. Thus, the mistreatment of women by the other community aims to humil-
iate and also produce asymmetrical power dynamics between the perpetrator
and the 'dishonoured' community. Shweta Kushal and Evangeline Manickam also
focus on the othering process and discuss that it becomes even more significant

---

347 Beth Baron, 'Women, Honour, and the State: Evidence from Egypt', *Middle Eastern Studies*, 42, 1 (2006), pp. 1–20, p. 1.

348 Namrata Mitra, 'Shamed Bodies: Partition Violence and Women', in *The Female Face of Shame*, ed. by Erica L. Johnson and Patricia Moran (Bloomington, IN: Indiana UP, 2013), p. 199.

349 Ibid., p. 205.

in diasporic communities to identify national borders through the reproduction of honour codes. Women are required to preserve the ethnic identity and to 'act as the custodians of ethnicity because, in a migrant condition, ethnicity plays out more in the realm of the community or the home which in turn is the domain of the women. [T]he physical fact of a woman's body is marked with the boundaries that symbolise ethnicity and cultural codes'.[350] The norms of honour and shame are reinforced within diasporic communities to distinguish the self from the other. Thus, honour and shame become the markers of identity through which the forms of national and ethnic differences such as gender roles, religious and traditional practices are reproduced.

In reproducing traditional values, I suggest that the veil gains an important position. As the veil has multiple connotations, it can also be described as a boundary marker between honour and shame. The veil gains a subversive quality as it challenges and subverts the colonial gaze and national borders. Through the creative use of the veil, Algerian women re-familiarised with their bodies. The veil, which was familiar and defined as backward and old-fashioned within a colonial Algerian context, becomes unfamiliar and a tool of camouflage during the war, and thus helping Algerian women transgress national and gendered boundaries.[351] Here, I concentrate on how the process of (un)veiling is related to the concepts of honour and shame. When the veil is defined as a symbol of oppression for women who are othered, the practice of (un)veiling gains a subversive quality. Bahar Davary focuses on different practices of veiling and questions to what extent the veil can be liberating or shaming. The veil usually connotes religiosity, modesty and submission to norms of sexual purity and fidelity, as discussed by Davary.[352] However, the veil is re-defined in different contexts as honourable or shaming. Davary discusses how the Turkish national revolution in the early twentieth century designed the new national state by re-defining the image of a new 'Turkish woman', who was unveiled, modern and westernised, but almost too asexual in the public sphere.[353] On the other hand, veiling has still been practised and seen as backward by some political groups until the present day. The conservative part of Turkish society also defined unveiling as

350 Shweta Kushal, and Evangeline Manickam, '(Dis)honourable Paradigms: A Critical Reading of Provoked, Shame and Daughters of Shame', South Asian Diaspora, 6, 2 (2014), pp. 225–38, p. 228.
351 I have a more detailed discussion of the veil in a colonial context in Chapter 2.
352 Davary, 'Miss Elsa and the Veil', p. 49.
353 Fatma Müge Göçek, Political Cartoons in the Middle East (Princeton, NJ: Markus Wiener Publishers, 1998), p. 14.

dishonourable and shaming as they regarded the practice of veiling as one of female purity. This suggests that the veil holds different meanings and that both meanings are constructed as binary opposites, remaining and just as confining. Davary argues that wearing the veil and Western attire together demonstrates a new system of veiling, which deflects both binary opposites of honour and shame. The new system of veiling regarding honour and shame, Davary discusses, is based on 'their desire to redefine one's identity as a Turkish woman'.[354] As the veil is related to the patriarchal ideals of chastity and modesty for women, a woman may be veiled just to 'be invisible' in the society.[355] Therefore, the veil may gain a subversive quality to divert the unwanted male gaze and works to deflect unwanted attention. At the same time, wearing westernised clothing may suggest conforming to the ideals of the Turkish revolution. Pnina Werbner defines the veil as 'an embodied guarantor of personal modesty'.[356] As the veil has been long associated with discussions of modesty, Werbner claims that it falls within the complex of honour and shame.[357] Werbner argues that the adoption of a new form of veiling is 'a cunning solution invented by young people themselves to *appear* to honour their parents (and to defy others in positions of authority) while nevertheless demanding the right to decide their own destiny'.[358] Wearing the veil gives them the disguise to *appear* honourable and attain the right to their bodies. This also reminds us of how the veil was re-defined in a colonial context as a form of camouflage. Here, young people transgress the boundaries of honour and shame which were pre-defined by patriarchal and religious authorities by seeming to follow those ideals. It therefore deflects the attention on their bodies so they can transform the social and gender boundaries within which they were previously restricted. The novel critiques how shame and honour are always constructed as binary concepts that restrict women in a limited space. The text explores shame with an analogy of the colour white:

> It was all because women were made of the lightest cambric, [...] whereas men were cut of thick, dark fabric. That is how God had tailored the two: one superior to the other. [T]he colour black didn't show stains, unlike the colour white, which revealed even the

---

354 Davary, 'Miss Elsa and the Veil', p. 64.

355 Ibid., p. 60.

356 Pnina Werbner, 'Veiled interventions in Pure Space: Honour, Shame and Embodied Struggles among Muslims in Britain and France', *Theory, Culture and Society*, 24, 2 (2007), pp. 161–86, p. 174.

357 Ibid., p. 178.

358 Ibid., p. 179, emphasis in original.

tiniest speck of dirt. By the same token, women who were sullied would be instantly noticed and separated from the rest, like husks removed from grains.

'[H]onour' was more than a word. It was also a name. You could call your child 'Honour', as long as it was a boy. Men had honour. Old men, middle-aged men, even schoolboys so young that they still smelled of their mothers' milk. Women did not have honour. Instead, they had shame. And, as everyone knew, Shame would be a rather poor name to bear.[359]

This extract is narrated as a monologue by a mother to her daughters to maintain patriarchal boundaries of femininity. Here, the colour white represents purity which is predisposed to be marked by any act that disrupts the chastity of a woman just as the colour white would show any speck of dirt. Likewise, the text demonstrates how society constructs femininity as fragile and shameful. The text uses many analogies of colour in relation to women. As I suggest in the following section, wearing a white piece of clothing instead of red becomes a woman's silent protest of her innocence. In contrast, masculinity is always associated with honour and the colour black while women are denied access to honour even in the abstract sense. Women would need to be chaste and strictly distanced from sexuality and desires to protect the family honour while men are not expected to be chaste or sexually pure. Paul Gilbert discusses how '[c]ontrol of female sexuality (and the female body) has been institutionalised in social and religious forms for hundreds of years and [...] often involving the shaming/stigmatising of female sexuality and appearance'.[360] The social stigmatisation of shame has the power to undermine feminine sexuality and thus effectively rendering women's identities 'non-existent'. This binary opposition does not recognise femininity or allow women to have a voice for their bodies and sexualities. Whilst men are removed from this opposition with honour regardless of age or actions, only women are expected to embody shame by society based on their experiences and dictated by the patriarchal norms that control women's bodies.

I argue that the novel works to undermine the binary opposition of shame and honour by manipulating the boundaries of femininity and shame in the novel. Similar to Cixous's urging women to write in order to reclaim the dominant narrative discourse, the novel explores the concepts of honour and shame together to reclaim the honour they have been denied access. The text interrogates how

---

359 Shafak, *Honour*, p. 16.
360 Paul Gilbert, 'Body Shame: A Biopsychosocial Conceptualisation and Overview with Treatment Implications', in *Body Shame: Conceptualisation, Research and Treatment*, ed. by Paul Gilbert and Jeremy Miles (Hove and New York: Brunner-Routledge, 2002), p. 35.

these concepts could be undermined by embracing and incorporating silence and shame into the reproduction of femininity. Postcolonial feminine writing is this re-imagining of honour and shame as unstable rather than a fixed position for women. It offers a new perspective to re-interpret honour and shame as a repeated process. Thus, I suggest that these norms are not binary opposites. Rather, they constitute the potential of power when they are re-interpreted as a process of (un)veiling. I analyse the norms of honour and shame as (un)veiling because they can be used to help women transgress boundaries by seeming to conform to these boundaries. Although shame is supposed to be a restrictive position for women, if manipulated, it can create a temporary shift in power dynamics.

The interrogation of these binary oppositions of honour/shame through the colours black/white in the novel are reminiscent of Cixous's interrogation of binary oppositions in 'Sorties'. Cixous explores how the process of thinking and of social norms are dependent on binary oppositions which appropriate the self with regards to the other. She further argues that this othering system constructs the feminine as non-existent and unthinkable. Cixous writes:

> Where is she?
> Activity/passivity
> Sun/Moon
> Culture/Nature
> Day/Night
> Father/Mother
> [...]
> <u>Man</u>
> Woman
> Always the same metaphor: we follow it, it carries us, beneath all its figures, wherever discourse is organized. [O]rganization by hierarchy makes all conceptual organizations subject to man. Male privilege [is] shown in the opposition between activity and passivity. [...] Either woman is passive or she does not exist. What is left of her is unthinkable, unthought.[361]

Here, Cixous questions several systems of binary oppositions and demonstrates how this hierarchy between honour/shame, along with 'activity/passivity', 'man/woman' and similarly 'West/East', tends to define the position of women in a limited space and without voice. Women's existence, which is defined by passivity, becomes possible only in these pre-defined terms. Likewise, the honour/shame dichotomy depends on limiting women's existence into the space of shame and

---

361 Cixous, 'Sorties', pp. 37–9.

so does not recognise their voices other than through this lens. Timothy Bewes argues that '[postcolonial] shame appears in the gap between the impossibility of speaking and the impossibility of not speaking'.[362] The binary opposition of voice and silence, speaking and not speaking, is an impossible position which highlights 'male privilege' and undermines the existence of the other to the normative male form. Reproducing the same binary also works to undermine the voices of the other and therefore produces postcolonial shame. Postcolonial feminine writing re-imagines the voice and the existence of women from within the binary. While speech is reflected as an impossibility, when, restricted within the binary opposition, silence is also a potentially untenable position. Postcolonial feminine writing interrogates the possibility of agency for women by exploring silence and shame, which are assumed to restrict women. While the dominant narrative discourse limits women's speech, silence also presents a challenge for women to overcome. Therefore, it becomes necessary to rework these norms for women to re-connect to their bodies and voices.

I want to capture how *Honour* has been analysed by other critics and to contextualise the difference of my own argument before moving on with my discussion of the novel. *Honour* has been a popular novel specifically because it highlights issues of honour killings, oppression against women and relating migration. In doing so, one would expect that this novel would merely offer insight into the East and Eastern practices of (family) honour; but the novel particularly transgresses East/West boundaries by re-writing plural identities. On the one hand, Tatiana Golban contextualises *Honour* as a migrant novel and focuses on the boundaries of masculine honour codes with Alex as the migrant hero. Golban considers how Alex 'oscillates between two different cultures, between his different identities; he fluctuates between the liberated, free man [and] his image of himself' which is predominantly constructed upon the 'superiority of the male role'.[363] In doing so, Golban suggests the possibility of a hybrid and multiple identity for Alex, who represents this by embracing different social norms for his home (as Iskender) and his English girlfriend (as Alex). Although Golban mentions the fluidity of Alex's name, she does not consider how Alex can regulate his behaviour based on this name change. As the son of a migrant, a

362 Timothy Bewes, *The Event of Postcolonial Shame* (Princeton, NJ: Princeton UP, 2011), p. 40.
363 Tatiana Golban, 'The Migrant Hero's Boundaries of Masculine Honour Code in Elif Shafak's *Honour*', in *Culture, Literature and Migration*, ed. by Ali Tilbe, and Rania M. Rafik Khalil (London: Transnational Press, 2019), pp. 103–18, pp. 114–5.

half-Turkish and half-Kurdish family in London, Alex has the ability to reinvent his identity as the very boundaries between Askander/Iskender/Alexander seem fluid and transforming.

On the other hand, Petya Tsoneva Ivanova offers insightful arguments on *Honour* and Shafak's border-crossing position. Ivanova considers *Honour* a contemporary Alexander re-write as the novel is centred on Alex, who is raised as the 'sultan' of the house.[364] Ivanova makes transnational and transgenerational observations between Alexander the Great and Alex. In doing so, Ivanova suggests that Shafak 'restore[s] a lost Middle East to itself [and] relocate[s] Turkey, Europe and North America/the US along fluid borderlines in literary heterotopias where the West can recover its "Easternness" and the East – its "Westernness" '.[365] This is a very significant argument as it highlights how Shafak complicates and therefore crosses East/West borders successfully in her narrative. Furthermore, Ivanova suggests that this becomes Shafak's way of inscribing postcolonialism in her novels. Along similar lines to my discussion in my Introduction, Ivanova argues that Turkey's Westernisation process enacted by Turkish founding fathers does not suggest a case of active colonisation; however, it demonstrates Western impact on the modern Turkish state and its then contemporary legal codes. I agree with Ivanova in that Shafak does not attempt to open 'the East to Western reformulation', but she makes border-crossing possible by creating plural and hybrid, and in some cases, migrant identities.[366] Particularly because she attempts to elaborate and reclaim a multiplicity of identities in her various novels including *The Gaze* and *Honour*, I would suggest Shafak creates 'fluid borderlines' in her novels while preferring hybridity over nationalistic views.[367] Although Ivanova provides an insight into the use of silences in the novel, she does not particularly indicate the potentials of silence in the text. Conversely, I incorporate the norms of speech and silence, and honour and shame to my concept of postcolonial feminine writing because they offer a new way of interpreting social and gender norms in *Honour*. I particularly argue that femininity is re-structured in the novel. To demonstrate this, I offer a close reading of the novel in relation to the themes of silence and speech, and honour

---

364 Alex's mother repeatedly addresses Alex as her 'sultan'.
365 Ivanova, *Negotiating Borderlines*, pp. 168–9.
366 Ibid., p. 169.
367 Ibid., p. 169.

and shame. This allows me to show how bodies become means of communication and resistance that defy the constraints placed on women's bodies through social oppression and shame.

Embodied Speech: Re-imagining Women's Silences and Voices

Honour explores how the notions of speech and silence undermine dominant patriarchal discourses. As Proma Tagore discusses, silence is not merely the absence of speech.[368] Indeed, silence becomes a tool in this context to refuse these patriarchal restraints. Postcolonial feminine writing allows silence to be an alternative to dominant narratives and potentially undermines patriarchal and imperial interventions. The text embraces speech and silence together in a fragmented narrative. By focusing on silence, the novel calls the dominance of voice into question. Shafak recognises the significance of women's various acts of silences and thanks women who shared their stories but also their *silences* with her for *Honour*.[369] Kamala Visweswaran argues that it is significant to listen not only to 'women's speech, but women's silences as well'.[370] Here, silence is explored as a concept of communication and a site of resistance to dominant narrative and patriarchal discourses. By listening to women's silences, Visweswaran argues that we may learn different strategies of resistance.[371] Donna McCormack argues that silence is not 'an absence of communication – in contrast to dominant (and negative) interpretations of silence – it is a call for an intimate listening and thus for a different form of being with others'.[372] I agree with McCormack in that the imaginative use of silence as a form of communication interrogates how knowledge is re-produced within dominant narrative discourses.[373] While silence effectively undermines dominant power structures by resisting the reproduction of them, it also provides an alternative to dominant narrative discourses. Therefore, silence necessitates a different form of listening. Similarly, Cheryl Glenn argues that 'silence *as a rhetoric*, as a constellation of symbolic strategies […] serves

---

368 Proma Tagore, *The Shapes of Silence* (Montreal and Kingston: McGill-Queen's UP, 2009), p. 142.

369 Shafak, *Honour*, p. 343.

370 Kamala Visweswaran, *Fictions of Feminist Ethnography* (Minneapolis, MN: The University of Minnesota Press, 1994), p. 31.

371 Ibid., p. 31.

372 McCormack, *Queer Postcolonial Narratives*, p. 45.

373 Ibid., p. 45.

many functions' that 'can deploy power [or] defer to power'.[374] Thus, the novel invites the reader to read and listen to these silences intimately.

In considering how 'speech and silence depend upon each other', it is useful to turn back to the *Nights*. Here, Shahrazad controls both voice and silence by repeating a cycle of storytelling similar to the process of (un)veiling.[375] Each tale is closed by remarking: '[m]orning overtook Scheherazade, [...] and she lapsed into silence'.[376] Where the night is dominated by Shahrazad's voice, the day is similarly marked by her silence. Shahrazad's storytelling is veiled under layers of multiple narrators and voices throughout the night and unveiled again in the morning as a form of feigned subordination to the King. The repeated process of (un)veiling unsettles social and gender norms by playing into them. Before Shahrazad's literary intervention, the King's rule confined his wives' lives into a day/night binary, which enforced silence and death on them. Shahrazad's story-telling changes the significance of the binary opposition of day/night just as the veil is re-interpreted through (un)veiling. Shahrazad begins each tale at night to cease narrating at the dawn and she feigns silence to wait for the King's verdict on her life. Here, storytelling follows the same process of repetition: Shahrazad's silence is strategic and aims to manipulate dominant power structures. By not giving her voice over to the King's control, Shahrazad incorporates silence into her cycle of tales as a technique of narrative, which forms suspense and gives her the power to withhold her voice when it is most expected to conform. This form of narrative, when repeated or borrowed in newer literary forms, is the literary concept I describe as postcolonial feminine writing. Shahrazad's voice is enacted and empowered by instances of silence. Therefore, postcolonial feminine writing allows me to explore silences as that which enable communication and, in some cases, allow other women's voices to emerge. Radha Hegde argues that 'agency can be viewed as the locus from which action can be initiated, whether the action is of resistance or reconfirmation [i]f the resistance is, indeed, at the core of agency'.[377] Here, the action of silence is 'at the core of agency' as it is initiated from resistance. In contrast to dominant interpretations of silence as negative and limiting, I would suggest that silence can be a form of communication that

---

374 Cheryl Glenn, *Unspoken: A Rhetoric of Silence* (Carbondale, IL: Southern Illinois UP, 2004), p. 18, emphasis in original.
375 Ibid., p. 7.
376 Mernissi, *Scheherazade*, p. 45.
377 Radha S. Hegde, 'Narratives of Silence: Rethinking Gender, Agency, and Power from the Communication Experiences of Battered Women in South India', *Communication Studies*, 47, 4 (1996), pp. 303–17, p. 310.

is an alternative language for women to speak through without conforming to patriarchal boundaries. Indeed, I would insist that having a voice is not always liberating. Speech may become a restrictive form if it re-iterates dominant narrative and patriarchal discourses. *Honour* shows how postcolonial feminine writing can transgress the patriarchal narrative discourse and re-define it from within.

The novel re-imagines silence as a site of resistance. Jamila, one of the twin sisters, was kidnapped when she was a teenager, and as a result the taboo of her virginity becomes a public issue. This issue is relayed to the reader and Adem, who asked for Jamila's hand in marriage, through the voice of the village head. By seeing this memory from the village head's perspective instead of Jamila's, the reader witnesses how Jamila resists the patriarchal order by maintaining silence about her body and virginity. This reveals how the codes of honour and shame are constituted and maintained by patriarchy. The village head states that 'her father beat her several times but still not a word. A midwife examined her. She says Jamila has no hymen but some girls are born like this'.[378] Her 'honour' depends on her keeping her virginity intact and it becomes a public shame for the family when her virginity is questioned. Jamila is not allowed to have a voice in relation to her body. Instead, she is forced to have a virginity test, which is an intrusion into her body and a symbolic rape that reproduces the patriarchal order. The public intervention as to how Jamila's body is defined creates a distance between her body and her voice. Therefore, she maintains silence even in the face of extreme violence. Jamila's refusal to speak is an act of resistance to the dominant language boundaries within which she is expected to speak. By confirming or denying claims surrounding her virginity, she would have to re-iterate the patriarchal language. Rather, she rejects these boundaries around her voice by maintaining silence.

Here, I want to turn to Fanon because he not only provides a basis for my theorising of postcolonial feminine writing in terms of Algerian women's imaginative use of the veil in their fight for liberation, but also proposes as a significant method of resistance. He examines the case of a French colonial agent, who interrogates Algerian freedom fighters. Fanon quotes the agent:

> Sometimes we almost wanted to tell them that if they had a bit of a consideration for us they'd speak out without forcing us to spend hours tearing information word by word out of them. But you might as well speak to the wall. To all the questions we asked they'd only say 'I don't know'. Even when we asked what their name was. [...] Of course there

---

378 Shafak, *Honour*, p. 97.

are some that don't scream; those are the tough ones. [T]hey don't make things easy for us.[379]

This extract shows how an act of silence may become a form of resistance. To resist the interrogation, the Algerian prisoners deploy silence which proves to be significant and powerful in this context because the agent needs the prisoner to speak and to listen to what he says. However, the prisoners will lose their voices in this hierarchy even if they speak. Here, the prisoners hold a position of 'the impossibility of speaking and the impossibility of not speaking'.[380] Therefore, they only maintain silence as a resistance to colonial violence. The agent recognises that those who do not even scream while being tortured are 'the tough ones'. I would go further and suggest that the patriarchal order is inextricably linked to colonial violence through the way it imposes speech and silence on women who are othered. The text explores Jamila as a silent freedom fighter in this context because of her position as a Kurdish woman in Turkey. Jamila is from a family of Kurdish descent, and Jamila and Pembe are the only girls who can speak Turkish because they attended a Turkish-educated primary school. The novel clarifies how Kurdish women are doubly-oppressed in this context as it is significantly more difficult for them to access education, primarily because of the language barrier, as well as gender and economic issues. The text shows how gender and ethnicity operate mutually to impose an intersectional oppression on Jamila. Similar to a colonial prisoner, Jamila experiences violence during the interrogation, but she never answers a question on her virginity. Her voice would only replicate the patriarchal terms. Speech would be damaging and would further render her voice worthless after it is spoken since her words would need to be spoken in the paternal language that constrains her voice. Alternatively, Jamila's voice would fall on 'the deaf male ear, which hears in language only that which speaks in the masculine'.[381] Her speech that deviates from these predefined terms would not be heard or listened to. Furthermore, this form of silence suggests the desire to protect her body and voice. The novel deliberately undermines the patriarchal authority by withholding her voice which does not 'make things easy' for them. By seeming to conform to patriarchal interpretations as an act of docility, silence is a postcolonial feminine writing technique as it undermines the search for knowledge about a woman's body.

---

379 Frantz Fanon, *The Wretched of the Earth*, trans. by Constance Farrington (London: Penguin, 2001), pp. 213–4.

380 Bewes, *Postcolonial Shame*, p. 40.

381 Cixous, 'Medusa', pp. 880–1.

I would suggest that silence is a liberating concept, which undoes the patriarchal society presented in the novel. Jamila's silence is therefore an act of agency as well as a form of communication, which holds the power to share or withhold her voice. Before Adem learned about Jamila's past, she was open with affection and concern for him.[382] After he confronts her about her side of the story in anger, reproaching her with shame, 'Jamila's stare hardened'.[383] Adem tells Jamila that her father shared with Adem that she may not be a virgin, to which she replies with restraint and avoiding his eyes: 'Adem had expected her to react more dramatically, protesting in the face of such insolence, crying her heart out. But she was oddly composed as she raised her head and looked at him'.[384] He speaks to Jamila in a demanding voice, which results in the reinforcement of a gender hierarchy. McCormack argues that this type of silence needs a more 'intimate' form of listening and reading bodily gestures, which Adem does not have the capacity for.[385] His inability to form this intimate listening indicates the inadequacy of patriarchal dominant discourses in recognising women's speech. Although Jamila's initial reaction could be read as feeling shame due to the aversion of her eyes, as she quickly regains her tentative pose. This suggests that Jamila 'speak[s] with, through and on' her body, integrating voice and silence together to communicate her language.[386] Here, Jamila follows a pattern of speech and silence as exercised by Shahrazad. Her composure along with her response to Adem that of '[t]he truth is what you make of it' reveals that her voice is not simply absent.[387] She does not share her voice with people who aim to restrain it. Cixous argues, '[s]he doesn't "speak", she throws her trembling body forward; she lets go of herself, she flies; all of her passes into her voice, and it's with her body that she vitally supports the "logic" of her speech'.[388] This offers an insight into liberating women's speech. Cixous shows how a woman can actively use her body to support and 'materialise' her speech, and thus the woman is able to develop her own voice. In the novel, Jamila's silent reactions and bodily poses communicate that she reserves the right to speak about her own body. She therefore develops a form of communication that displays the vitality of her voice.

---

382 Shafak, *Honour*, p. 92.
383 Ibid., p. 92.
384 Ibid., p. 98.
385 McCormack, *Queer Postcolonial Narratives*, p. 45.
386 Ibid., p. 181.
387 Shafak, *Honour*, p. 99.
388 Cixous, 'Medusa', p. 881.

By refusing to speak and say what is expected of her as embodied by her father, Jamila forms a language of silence that conveys her resistance. Sara Ahmed argues that certain types of communication do not necessarily require the presence of a recognised voice, 'precisely because [it] open[s] an unfinished, unheard history, which cannot be fully presented, even if it is not absent'.[389] This form of communication thus shows the existence of a postcolonial feminine language even if it fails to be heard by the patriarchal authorities. Here, the fact that this language is not recognised by the patriarchal figures is empowering because it penetrates into the pre-defined language constraints precisely like (un)veiling. Her silence conveys the presence of an unvoiced history, which could not be represented even if it was voiced. If Jamila confirms their suspicions on her body, it will not only limit her position in the society, but it will break her connection to her body as well. In contrast, silence allows her to re-acquaint herself with her body as well as her voice because (un)veiling voice is specifically a form of postcolonial feminine resistance. Her silence becomes an irreducible quality specifically because it further allows her freedom and agency. The text suggests that her role as a midwife, who 'survive[s] on her own in the wilderness', does not conform to patriarchal norms of femininity.[390]

The text uses space to undermine pre-defined gender roles. Jamila's cellar is one of the most important spaces in the novel that allows her to replace speech with different forms of communication. In other words, the cellar is a liminal space that allows Jamila to speak through her healing potions. She is a well-known midwife and a healer. Her liminality is explained by her interpretation of the villagers' image of her as a 'witch who paced the tightrope between two worlds'.[391] She is therefore described as a silent character who embodies different forms of communication and 'speaks with and through' her body.[392] The cellar is a space that endorses her silence through different senses:

> When Jamila was in the cellar, she stepped outside of her body, becoming a conduit of an arcane energy that coursed through the universe, healing, mending, multiplying. There she gave birth to her own womb, and the womb expanded to cover the whole of the natural world around her, a cavern of warmth and compassion, in which she happily lost all sense of self. She could never tell whether it was night or day. [...] She lived outside of the clock in a cycle of her own. [A] distinct, earthy, pungent smell lingered in the air,

---

389 Sara Ahmed, *Strange Encounters*, p. 156.
390 Shafak, *Honour*, p. 173.
391 Ibid., p. 173.
392 McCormack, *Queer Postcolonial Narratives*, p. 181.

although Jamila was no longer able to detect it. If a stranger went down there however, he would become giddy, overwhelmed by the odour.[393]

The cellar is a space outside normative boundaries of time and space.[394] There, her bodily form is disintegrated into a pregnant mystified manifestation of energy embracing the whole universe. The cellar becomes her womb which again gives birth to a new Jamila every time she steps into it. Her communication with the universe develops into a language of 'warmth and compassion'. The text suggests that Jamila can develop her other senses because of the change in her bodily form in the cellar. Here, the senses become an alternative form of communication, which I am calling postcolonial feminine as they do not conform to a colonial or patriarchal order. Jamila is able to control her own senses to communicate with the 'natural world around her' in a way that goes beyond the dominant use of speech. This allows her to find a 'hidden crossover' through her body to express her existence and voice. Therefore, the senses become the means through which Jamila communicates with other living forms. The cellar sustains a 'pungent' odour which overwhelms strangers. In relation to *Cereus Blooms at Night*, McCormack discusses how the protagonist's garden becomes a way of remembering her colonial and incestuous traumas and an invitation to keep the memories alive as '[t]hese odours bring forth traces of memories unavailable in other forms. [...] Smell is the *body's* way of remembering'.[395] Similarly, Jamila tries to keep her past alive by developing her senses in the cellar. This suggests the existence of an intricate form of communication within the cellar, which cannot be accessed by others. I would argue that this type of language is postcolonial feminine specifically because it refuses to reproduce the patriarchal norms while forming a connection between the body and communication. The novel suggests that seeing is more than a bodily sense as it is a sort of language for Jamila: 'Jamila was a seer [...] who spoke the language of birds, reptiles and insects'.[396] Sight also refers to her ability to form extra sensory perception. In this way, the text purposely re-appropriates the term 'witch' by exploiting the witch/woman dichotomy. Here, there is an undeniable resemblance between

---

393 Shafak, *Honour*, pp. 172–3.
394 Julia Kristeva gives useful insight into how women experience time in cycles and different than men in 'Women's Time'. However, I choose not to engage with Kristeva's essay to keep my focus on women's language and narrative, as per my overall and specific arguments, instead of time and space.
395 McCormack, *Queer Postcolonial Narratives*, pp. 51–2, emphasis in original.
396 Shafak, *Honour*, pp. 172–3.

Jamila and Medusa. In 'Medusa', Cixous re-imagines Medusa as a laughing woman refuting Medusa's previous image as deadly and horrific. Medusa shows both the very feminine and the very horrifying qualities of embodiment for the patriarchal authority. It is her body and specifically her head through which she communicates. By re-defining Medusa as laughing, rather than deadly, Cixous draws attention to how the recognition of Medusa's communication depends on a new way of looking at and reading her. Similarly, this re-definition of Jamila as a witch/woman presents her capability to perform communicative acts stemming from her body. The body has a language of its own that refuses to be restricted to the supremacy of voice. Therefore, it becomes another system of knowledge through which the binary systems are deconstructed.

The novel reveals how voice is not always liberating for women, particularly when women's voices reproduce restrictive patriarchal norms. Although Pembe is employed and outspoken, her voice is not liberating. I suggest that her voice needs to go through the process of (un)veiling to enable its liberation because the repetition of her voice by multiple narrators undoes the patriarchal constraints on it. The novel shows that Pembe replicates the codes of honour and shame that she learned from her mother and that she passes on to Esma. The text suggests that Pembe becomes more patriarchal in time by further restricting her daughter's life while enabling Alex's life. Esma talks about her experience with her mother:

> We had been very close, me and my mother, but all that changed the moment my breasts started to bud and I had my first period. The only thing she was interested in now was my *virginity*. She was always preaching about the things I should never/ ever/ not even in my wildest dreams do. [...] Yet she didn't impose the same rules on my brothers. [W]ith Iskender she was totally different, open. Iskender didn't need to be careful. He could just be himself.[397]

Pembe's language reiterates the patriarchal language she was taught earlier by her mother. While Esma's virginity should be protected at all costs, Iskender is let free by their mother. Pembe's relationship with her daughter becomes more restricting as Esma develops more feminine features and her value in society is confined to the taboo of her virginity. Specifically because Pembe's language reiterates and reproduces pre-defined gender and social codes, her voice limits not only Esma, but herself as well. Kushal and Manickam agree 'the code of honour is passed on silently and girls learn it at an early age [that] honour crimes and beatings are common, which in turn help reinforc[e] the code'.[398] Pembe

---

397 Shafak, *Honour*, pp. 184–5.
398 Kushal, and Manickam, '(Dis)honourable paradigms', p. 233.

replicates the codes of honour and shame by teaching the same norms to her daughter. Pembe is freed from her patriarchal ideologies after witnessing her son's crime. Since her relatives believe Pembe is dead, she disappears from her home and goes to Jamila's village home to replace her life. By abandoning her family for Jamila's isolated village, Pembe symbolically dies alongside Jamila. Pembe's voice is liberated only after her symbolic death as she becomes isolated in Jamila's home and writes letters to her daughter. Since Pembe speaks within a language that reinforces her body and voice to become restricted, her voice is never really heard, and she is symbolically silenced. Compared to Jamila's silence which is voluntary and resistant, Pembe's voice is initially limited. Nevertheless, the text gives her voice another chance through her daughter.

I would argue that Esma mimics Shahrazad in *Honour* with her role as the storyteller as she gives a voice to her mother's and aunt's stories. Esma grows up in London with her mother's strict patriarchal codes. Following a Shahrazadean tradition of storytelling, Esma uses silence and speech to empower her voice. Esma differs from both Pembe and Jamila in the way she brings together voice and silence to liberate herself, her mother and her aunt. In contrast to Pembe, whose voice reproduces patriarchal gender codes, and Jamila who embraces silence due to her past trauma, Esma becomes the designated narrator who listens attentively to their stories and narrates their pains on their *behalf*.[399] Pembe tells Esma that she always supports snails, the weaker side, and so she is a snail herself. However, Esma deliberately supports the weaker side in the binary. While Shahrazad takes a position to protect other powerless women against the King, Esma supports people whom she considers weaker, such as her mother, by narrating their perspectives in her stories. The text clarifies Esma's position with regards to patriarchy as she begins narrating her mother's story before her brother's release from prison. This shows the desire to speak and tell stories that cannot be interrupted by the patriarchal figures as her brother symbolises the patriarchy at home for her. As she speaks about woman and 'bring[s] woman to [her] writing', her voice attains a change of perspective in narration.[400] Cixous suggests that when women write, they 'proclaim this unique empire so that other women, other unacknowledged sovereigns, might exclaim: I, too over-flow'.[401] Building on Cixous's conception, I would argue that Esma 'proclaims'

399   Elaine Scarry, *The Body in Pain: The Making and Unmaking of the World* (Oxford: Oxford UP, 1985), p. 6.

400   Cixous, 'Medusa', p. 875.

401   Ibid., p. 876.

a previously unacknowledged state in her narration, and furthermore helps other women, particularly her mother and her aunt, pronounce their existences through her narration. This opens up the possibility of a subversive interruption in a long line of dominant and patriarchal narratives.

Alex recognises that Esma is different to their mother: 'Esma loved language. If someone used an expression she wasn't familiar with, she'd do anything to make it hers, like a collector who's found a coin'.[402] She dreams of becoming a writer and using a pen name which would be 'J. B. Ono [an amalgam of John Keats, William Blake and Yoko Ono]. A name for booksellers to mention in reverent tones. A bit mysterious and surely androgynous. A name in no need of a bra'.[403] While the amalgam of these names, it seems that Esma accepts the dominant masculine narrative initially, meaning that Esma aims to transgress the restrictive boundaries within which she has been raised. By picking an androgynous pen name, Esma commits a very gender non-conforming act. She aspires to transform the boundaries of dominant narrative discourse as a female writer. She thinks that 'female names were so different from male names, more whimsical and dreamlike, as if women were unreal, a figment of one's imagination', and she disregards this by incorporating Ono's name into her pen name.[404] Therefore, it is very significant that Esma pairs Ono's name, a Japanese-American female artist, with English canonical male poets. Esma undermines the standing of these canonical names by refusing to recognise an inherent hierarchy in gender, race or art forms. I would therefore suggest that she makes a very conscious decision to uphold Ono's name. Ono is well-known specifically for her *Cut Piece*, which is a passive and silent performance/protest against ageism, racism, sexism and violence.[405] Through this, she internalises the significance of silence into her narration. The search for a name that is 'in no need of a bra' is not a refusal of femininity. Rather, it suggests the desire to undermine the supposed inferiority of femininity. Furthermore, this suggests that social hierarchies are intersectional and require deconstructing simultaneously. Postcolonial feminine writing is therefore concerned with this deconstruction of social and gender hierarchies, which the text explores with Esma's attempt at re-naming herself. Whilst using Ono as her pen 'surname' along with only the initials of English canonical poets,

---

402 Shafak, *Honour*, p. 135.

403 Ibid., p. 183.

404 Ibid., p. 183.

405 Kevin Concannon, 'Yoko Ono's "Cut Piece": From Text to Performance and Back Again', *PAJ: A Journal of Performance and Art*, 30, 3 (2008), pp. 81–93, p. 83.

she intends to refute social and gender hierarchies and create a distinct language of her own, which mirrors Ono's art and nonverbal communication.

Esma's position of storyteller is recognised by Alex and mirrors Shahrazad's position. Her mother is so focused on the code of shame with regards to women that she only reproduces it. However, Esma speaks out and transgresses. Specifically, because her voice is different, Esma makes Alex 'listen' to her in the same way Shahrazad makes the King listen to her stories; whereas their mother is simply silenced. Here, the novel re-imagines the relationship between the King and Shahrazad as a sibling relationship.[406] As Alex is appointed 'the man of the house' after his father's departure, he impersonates the King. He effectively silences his mother by forbidding her to work outside the home. However, Alex realises that Esma is different in the way she uses language. Esma 'take[s] it in her own mouth, bite[s] that tongue with her very own teeth to invent for herself a language to get inside of'.[407] Esma is the storyteller because she makes the language hers and her difference is recognised by the patriarchal figure of the house. I suggest that her position is unique because she seems to conform to the patriarchal norms while she seeks to learn it, transform it and make it a language that she can 'get inside of'. Her voice is liberating because she does not reproduce the restrictive gender codes: 'snails were hermaphrodites, having both female and male reproductive organs. Why couldn't human beings be like that? If only God had modelled us on snails, there would be less heartbreak and agony in the world'.[408] She believes that transforming gender codes and being more androgynous – or hermaphrodite – would change the power dynamics between men and women, and honour and shame. Thus, she invents herself an androgynous pen name in order to re-create her identity and re-define her position in this hierarchy.

Esma considers gender differently from the restrictive patriarchal order her mother enforced. This reminds us of how Cixous suggests 'bisexuality' as a possibility of undermining the traditional masculine/feminine binary. Heterosexuality is the normative sexuality imposed by patriarchy and it restricts femininity in a pre-defined hierarchy. Cixous introduces the 'other bisexuality' as 'a third sex which is not reducible to either masculine or feminine but exceeds

---

406 Elsewhere, the text suggest that Iskender/Alex impersonates Shahrayar: '[i]n murdering one, Iskender has killed many'. Shafak, *Honour*, p. 331.

407 Cixous, 'Medusa', p. 887.

408 Shafak, *Honour*, p. 185.

both'.[409] Abigail Bray suggests that Cixous's understanding of 'other bisexuality' is an intervention in masculinity as men who 'inhabit the feminine through the passage of the "other" bisexuality will enter into a less violent relationship with the feminine'.[410] I would argue that Esma dreams of a similar gender non-conforming sphere where gender is not defined by patriarchy. The text shows how androgyny would deviate from the patriarchal order precisely by refusing to recognise an inherent gender hierarchy. The text suggests that gender hierarchy results in 'heartbreak and agony', which is a testimony to masculinity's 'violent relationship' with femininity. Postcolonial feminine writing here refuses the logic of masculinity as dominant, and constructs a narrative in which the androgynous body, by 'exceeding' both femininity and masculinity, deconstructs gender roles. This narrative deliberately refuses the heteronormative binary by interrogating religious patriarchal authority on the creation of humans as gendered and snails as hermaphrodite. I suggest that it is possible to re-imagine bodies as non-binary by focusing on the androgynous body as irreducible to the heteronormative binary. Furthermore, this text subverts categories of masculinity and femininity by playing with speech and silence. It explores voice and silence not as simply binary opposites, defined by the other, and therefore shows how speech and silence are forms of communication that repeat and complete each other. I explored how women's voices can be limiting when it replicates the patriarchal language, and silence is empowering as a site of resistance and refusal of the patriarchal language. Building on this undermining of the silence/voice binary, I want to concentrate on how the norms of honour and shame are reworked in relation to women's sexuality in the following section.

Shameful Sexuality: Challenging Patriarchal Norms of Femininity

Honour undermines the binary opposition of honour and shame by undoing the narrative of shame through the technique of repetition. Here, postcolonial feminine writing is the methodology for drawing out the links between shame, body and narrative. While shame is clearly depicted as a derogatory position for women, the text re-formulates how it manifests in women's identities. The focus is on how ideals of shame differ based on context, for example:

---

409   Abigail Bray, *Hélène Cixous: Writing and Sexual Difference* (Basingstoke: Palgrave Macmillan, 2004), p. 51.
410   Ibid., p. 51.

In England things were topsy-turvy. The word *couscous*, though ordinary was treated with reverence. Yet the word *shame*, though substantial, was taken quite lightly. When the English were disappointed about something, no matter how ephemeral or inconsequential, they exclaimed, 'Oh, what a shame!'[411]

Shame here is a contradictory image constructed as mundane in contrast to the novel's critique of embodying shame. Interpretations of the same concept vary from nation to nation. The text suggests that some words that exist in Turkish such as *couscous* and *shame* also have different meanings in English. Shame, as a word, becomes less influential and rather ordinary when used for exclamations and shows that the English language constructs an abstract sense of shame. Postcolonial feminine writing engages with the narrative of shame specifically because it is a social norm, which tends to restrict women in pre-defined boundaries. The norm of shame is undoubtedly gendered since it manifests differently for men and women. Eastern interpretations of shame, with regards to female sexuality, align with El Saadawi's discussion of 'keeping hymens intact'.[412] Patriarchal norms limit women's sexuality. Luce Irigaray argues that *the exchange of women between men establishes the order of a patriarchal society*. According to Irigaray, the social roles of mother, virgin and prostitute are imposed on women and therefore feminine sexuality is limited by the patriarchal society. Irigaray states that 'the properties of a woman's body have to be suppressed and subordinated to the exigencies of its transformation into an object of circulation of men'.[413] The woman's body has an 'expendable' value for the patriarchal economy as 'subordinated'. This suggests that women are restricted within the patriarchal order as sexual 'commodities'. *Honour* demonstrates how the patriarchal discourses use shame as a way of controlling women's sexualities and restricting their bodies within boundaries.

This novel explores an alternative interpretation of these social and gendered norms. Shame is not always a limiting position for women. The novel concentrates on Jamila's sexuality to explore a decline in her social position as a teenager because her virginity is doubted by the patriarchal authority. Her body becomes a source of public shame for her family. The patriarchal imposition of shame causes her excessive stress as she is exposed to domestic violence and a virginity test. However, Jamila uses this shame as an excuse for her liberation. She

411 Shafak, *Honour*, p. 283.
412 El Saadawi, *The Hidden Face of Eve*, p. 64.
413 Luce Irigaray, *This Sex Which Is Not One*, trans. by Catherine Porter (Ithaca, NY: Cornell UP, 1985), p. 187.

convinces her father to permit her to work as a midwife because the shameful position she was in suggests that she has not got any expendable value for the patriarchal economy. As the Virgin Midwife, she regains her dignified position in the community: 'the peasants didn't love her, but they did respect her. Travelling on horse, donkey and mule, she was allowed to set foot in places no other woman could enter. She was often accompanied by people she knew, but also by complete strangers'.[414] This suggests that Jamila embodies both shame and honour within her bodily experience. When the patriarchal authority renders her shameful, she seems to conform and uses it to transform her social and economic position. This implies a temporary shift of power dynamics between her and the patriarchal community. Whereas shame is supposed to weaken her social standing, it allows her to re-frame her sense of honour beyond the patriarchal impositions on her body. Shame allows her to depart from the prescribed path that has been laid out for her. In doing so, she is able to discover an alternative existence as a valuable subject apart from the patriarchal discourse designated for her. She re-discovers her honour as a midwife and so gains access to places and means of transport few women can. I would suggest that Jamila undoes the patriarchal boundaries of shame and honour by playing into these boundaries. She does not openly challenge these assumptions. Rather, she manipulates them into her own means. This creates a process of shame/honour similar to (un)veiling. She gains the ability to move across boundaries by conforming to both shame and honour simultaneously.

While the text focuses on both Jamila and Pembe's bodies to reflect the manifestation of shame in the patriarchal discourse, it also shows different stages of Pembe's sexuality such as virgin, mother and 'shameful' woman. She is represented as an ideal woman because of her unquestionable virginity when Adem, who previously expressed his love for Jamila, picks Pembe instead. This suggests, from a patriarchal perspective, that the norm of shame renders women susceptible to exchangeable commodities. Furthermore, Pembe's affair challenges this order and it is reflected through her delaying her 'motherly' duties at home. Yunus, the youngest son initially realises that their mother is different, 'withdrawn and lost in thought'.[415] Yunus thinks that '[a] few times she had forgotten to give him pocket money. And she also fed him less, not shoving as much food into his mouth, which is how Yunus knew something was definitely wrong. Pembe would never forget to feed him'.[416] Her 'fall' into shame is reflected as a fall

---

414 Shafak, *Honour*, p. 36.
415 Shafak, *Honour*, p. 62.
416 Ibid., p. 62.

from the position of motherhood. This suggests that the protection of honour primarily depends on how she conducts her role as a mother. Any indication of sexuality threatens the patriarchal order because it refuses the masculine order. Alex also shares his encounter with his mother and denounces her as guilty based on her movements: '[h]er lips were curved up in a smile, but her eyes were oddly sharp. I noticed a strand of hair had come out of her ponytail and one of the buttons in her white blouse was in the wrong hole'.[417] He interprets his mother's speech and movements as a display of shame as he *could sense her movements, touch her guilt, smell her shame*'.[418] Her dishevelled appearance implies for Alex that his mother is caught in an affair and therefore displays shame: '[t]hat's when I knew what Uncle Tariq had told me about my mother was true'.[419] The feelings of shame are reflected on the body by various facial expressions and her posture. While her tousled hair and blouse might indicate sexual intercourse/intimacy, her 'sharp' eyes do not immediately suggest shame or guilt. She looks directly at Alex and her smile suggests a touch of confidence contrary to her physical appearance. Here, the existence of shame entirely depends on its recognition by the patriarchal authority. Because the patriarchal discourse does not fully recognise femininity and women's sexuality, Alex's interpretation of his mother's sexuality is based on assumptions and simply replicates his uncle's statements. Here, shame serves to endorse the patriarchal discourse within which women's bodies are almost non-existent because they are only recognised in limited positions of 'mother, virgin or prostitute'. The narrative of shame contributes to the patriarchal control of women. However, such representations are disrupted through non-linear storytelling and the use of multiple narrative voices.

Postcolonial feminine writing 'un-writes' the narrative of shame by repeating it from the perspective of multiple narrators. Expanding on Fanon's discussion of the veil as a form of camouflage, I would like to draw out how (un)veiling is also a gender non-conforming disguise for the narrator's voice. The story of Pembe's affair is repeated by the narrator, whose voice is hidden under layers of narrators of different genders. By speaking in a male voice, the narrator critiques how the male voice has assumed supremacy. She uses the male voice to validate her honour all the while insinuating that the disguised voice belongs to Esma with hints only an insider would know: '[a] second later a key was thrust into the lock.

---

417 Ibid., p. 50.
418 Ibid., p. 51. The novel demonstrates that the norm of shame is a bodily experience that can be observed through multiple senses.
419 Ibid., p. 51.

[...] Only one person had his own key'.[420] While the perspective assumes a male voice, the narrator successfully demonstrates that she is still the 'mistress' of the narrative. This technique of storytelling is postcolonial feminine writing, insofar as it repeats both the themes and the techniques of narrative like Shahrazad, to create alternative and non-linear narratives. Shahrazad gradually eliminates the shame of the queen's adulterous story by turning the mirror back to the king. Similarly, Esma re-turns the mirror to his brother and the patriarchal society. She aims to deconstruct the story of her mother's shame by presenting different possibilities to explain her behaviour contrary to the patriarchal imposition of guilt.

Esma uses Elias's voice (Pembe's love interest) to explore her mother's story. This change in the narrative voice is a Shahrazadean technique as it disguises her voice and distances her perspective. Elias is a significant choice for the narrator to present because he does not readily follow the patriarchal norms. He is described as a cook, who '[is] a quarter Greek, a quarter Lebanese, a quarter Iranian and a quarter Canadian [and] had no problem with feeling like a foreigner because that is what he was in his heart: a stranger everywhere'.[421] His character suggests that he does not belong to any specific nation, and he also feels comfortable being a stranger. Here, Elias's identity defies any easy notion of national belonging. In addition, his work defies patriarchal expectations of men. As a chef, he works in the kitchen. This astounds Pembe because '[most] men [she] knew would barely enter the kitchen to get a glass of water for themselves'.[422] The text uses Elias's perspective to share Pembe's story because he already has a non-conforming identity. The narrator's appropriation of a male voice both appears to conform to patriarchal literary discourse and undermines it by providing a female perspective. As she demonstrates hospitality for her guest, she spills some hot tea on her crimson blouse, which she needs to change quickly with Elias there.[423] When Alex rings the bell, Pembe 'dash[es] out of her bedroom, her [white] blouse wrongly buttoned, [her face] horrified. [...] Elias signalled to her that he would hide [and] [t]hey exchanged tense whispers'.[424] Although the text does not specifically clarify the accuracy of either Alex's or Elias's stories, the passage undoes her assumed shame by framing her behaviour in a context that does not imply shame. This perspective runs counter to

---

420 Shafak, *Honour*, p. 290.
421 Ibid., p. 116.
422 Ibid., p. 117.
423 Ibid., p. 289.
424 Ibid., pp. 289–90.

the patriarchal narrative of shame and shows the inadequacy of the patriarchal discourse to interpret women's bodies. The text can transform the boundaries of shame from within the discourse because this narrator offers insight into the encounter as an alternative to the patriarchal interpretation. Therefore, the text re-imagines the same encounter that causes shame in Alex's interpretation as a form of shamelessness. Here, this act of re-narration is a refusal of shame, and thus shamelessness, because it does not simply reproduce shame as a result. The repetition creates a process of narrative through which shame ceases to exist. The narrator refuses to restrict her within the boundaries of shame by revealing the patriarchal perception as biased and pre-defined.

Pembe initially seems to conform to the patriarchal norms of honour by serving her guest tea and changing her clothes to appear respectfully. In contrast, the re-narrative reveals that the character displays shame not because she inherently feels it, but because the patriarchal authority restricts women to shame. The narrator disregards and un-writes this shame through the character's body. Pembe changes into a white blouse instead of the stained crimson one. The colour white is supposed to show stains easily and therefore symbolises women's innocence, which would be spoiled with any non-normative acts. The white blouse suggests a form of shaming misconduct and is a refusal to be constrained within the boundaries of shame. Here, the colour red is also symbolically stained by the patriarchal norms while donning the colour white on her body reflects her virtue publicly. It is because this shamelessness is reflected on and through her body that it is a powerful alternative to shame as 'to write from the body is to recreate the world'.[425] It not only undoes patriarchal interpretations of honour and shame, but it also suggests the possibility of repetition as a way of negating shame with shamelessness.

Conclusion

This chapter has argued that *Honour* (2012) is an example of the technique that I name postcolonial feminine writing. *Honour* bears striking resemblance to *The Gaze* (2006) in narrative style and content. The text maintains a fragmented writing style with multiple narrators and multiple voices. While Shafak narrated and re-narrated the same story with new, imaginative endings to 'undo' and redo the narrative content in *The Gaze*, she re-narrates the same story from

---

425 Ann Rosalind Jones, 'Writing the Body: Toward an Understanding of "L'Ecriture Feminine"', *Feminist Studies*, 7, 2 (1981), pp. 247–63, p. 252.

different perspectives in *Honour* to disrupt the dominant narrative discourses. The control of female sexuality has both private and public aspects which are defined by the norms of honour and shame. The novel explicitly criticises how honour always aligns with men, and women embody shame. Postcolonial feminine writing highlights how dominant narrative discourses tend to undermine women's existences by burying them in the gap of binary opposites, just as in the binary of honour and shame. The text interrogates this binary opposition and reveals that they are not stable norms. Therefore, by playing into these concepts, the novel invites the reader to take a stance and undermine the position of honour and shame to fluid social positions.

I have argued that the novel re-conceptualises the forms of silence and speech as different forms of communication. Contrary to the predominant understandings of silence as a lack of voice, and voice almost always defined with respect to power and authority, the novel re-imagines them as different components of communication. Silence is re-imagined as a site of resistance, a form of communication that requires an imaginative type of listening. Jamila is a silent freedom fighter who uses silence as a form of disguise to defy the imposition of shame on her body. While Jamila refuses to use the patriarchal language to define her virginity, her bodily form speaks for itself. While Jamila was interrogated on her virginity, given a virginity test, and publicly shamed due to her lack of a visible hymen, the reader learns her perspective from Esma's narrative rather than her defence, which otherwise would not be heard by 'the deaf male ear, which hears in language only that which speaks in the masculine'.[426] By working on silence, the predominance of voice is called into question. Although having voice is significant in some contexts (as Esma uses her voice), it may reproduce the gender and social norms that restrict women. When a voice goes unheard, it is no more liberated than a silenced victim. Esma, the character and the narrator of the novel, presents an alternative position to dominant narrative discourses. Esma uses both silence and voice to offer an insight into the perspectives of silent (Jamila) and silenced (Pembe) characters. Esma's character is constructed as an impersonation of Shahrazad and recognised differently because of her position as storyteller and her invitation to construct an androgynous world.

The text's portrayal of the concepts of honour and shame is an interrogation of patriarchal gender norms. The novel highlights the intricacy of these concepts by revealing how honour and shame change meaning in different social contexts. Honour and shame are social constructs and they do not inhabit stable positions.

---

426 Cixous, 'Medusa', pp. 880–1.

I have argued that the social categorisation of women by the patriarchal order depends predominantly on the norms of honour and shame. I have suggested that the repetition of the narrative of shame results in the refusal of shame by reiterating the story as shameless. Here, it indicates a way of overcoming patriarchal impositions of shame on women. However, the novel also offers new ways to re-imagine shame. Shame does not always restrict women. It is possible to manipulate the position of shame to gain access to shamelessness and this suggests feminine bodily experience that is denied by the patriarchal discourse.

Conclusion

Postcolonial Feminine Writing has argued that contemporary postcolonial women writers, such as al-Shaykh and Shafak employ what I call postcolonial feminine writing. This concept is particularly concerned with how patriarchal literary structures can be reworked from within. As such, this book interrogated the extent to which Shahrazad has been employed as a liberating figure in al-Shaykh and Shafak's novels. I wanted to suggest that postcolonial feminine writing employs the figure of Shahrazad to get within the patriarchal literary discourse in order to undo and re-think it. That is, Shahrazad uses her body to access a narrative voice and thus serves a significant position as the most prominent storyteller. In doing so, she controls both sexual desire and narrative desire. By defining the concept of postcolonial feminine writing at the intersections of Fanon's 'Algeria Unveiled', Cixous's 'Medusa' and Shahrazad's storytelling, I have tried to show the existence of multiple liberating spaces within narratives to which both writers made a claim by re-contextualising the voice and narrative techniques of Shahrazad the storyteller. Postcolonial feminine writing offers an alternative discourse to patriarchal and colonial discourses by constantly seeking ways to undermine and re-imagine them. For this reason, I suggested that Shafak and al-Shaykh follow and transcend Shahrazad's storytelling on multiple levels in *The Nights* (2011), *The Gaze* (2006) and *Honour* (2012).

Postcolonial feminine writing enables Shafak and al-Shaykh to re-create these liberating spaces in order to rethink patriarchal literary discourses as embodied, and to create forms, which challenge and re-imagine these embodied forms through Shahrazad's storytelling. As I discuss in Chapter I, several heteronormative bodies are repeatedly disrupted by acts of disguise/(un)veiling and alternative forms are suggested instead in *Nights*. This is most apparent when characters such as Zumurrud and the queen's slaves undermine patriarchal power structures by (un)veiling their bodies. Chapter I argued that bodies are already hybrid and plural, and indicated the fluidity of pre-defined patriarchal gender and social norms. While Chapter I explored the potential of voice and narrative by re-creating non-conforming bodies, Chapter II suggested that *The Gaze* employs marginalised/non-conforming characters (such as the fat woman and the Sable-Girl) to seize the potential of liberating spaces for multiple positions of the gaze. Chapter II argued that the position of the gaze is never stable, and thus such instability allows for re-imagining multiple gazing positions and enables the characters to be subjects of the gaze through the techniques of

Shahrazad's storytelling. By constantly re-imagining the same characters in different contexts, Chapter II demonstrated the potential of transforming narrative and bodily boundaries. Moving the focus from voice and gaze to the very corporeal body, Chapter III argued that postcolonial feminine writing allows for bodies to be expressive and liberating even if the voice is pre-dominantly patriarchal. I specifically examined how silence may be a liberating and subversive form of expression when it refuses to conform to patriarchal systems of power. In doing so, Chapter III demonstrated how bodies (and senses) become the means through which women speak in *Honour*. This does not mean that their voices are never heard. Postcolonial feminine writing allows for re-iterating these silent speeches through the voice of a narrator (Esma), who aimed to 'send [their stories] into some corner of the universe where [they] could float freely, away from [patriarchal authorities]', by specifically following a Shahrazadean practice of storytelling.[427] Therefore, I argued that postcolonial feminine writing provides the potential for women writers to develop a narrative of their own by replicating the prominent position of Shahrazad the storyteller, and thus resist and challenge the so-called silent and submissive positions of non-Western women.

By adopting both the title and tales of the longstanding Shahrazad's narrative, Chapter I aimed to exemplify the concept of postcolonial feminine writing. This novel revives the figure of Shahrazad within storytelling and re-writes her tales in a new order. Following a Shahrazadean tradition of enabling the other woman's voice (as does Shahrazad with her sister's question), al-Shaykh gives Shahrazad the potential to intervene in societal and gendered power structures and re-contextualises her narrative for contemporary readers. The *Nights* does not merely repeat these tales but re-formulates them to transform patriarchal power structures by allowing multiple narrators to gain their voices. As al-Shaykh becomes the 'mistress' of the tales, she reshapes the flow and the structure of the novel. Contradicting the previous adaptations of the *Nights*, al-Shaykh does not restrict this novel within pre-defined patriarchal literary boundaries. The novel ends by reciting the tale of Shahrazad and Shahrayar by another female narrator within the tales. Thus, in contrast to the European, male versions of the tales, the novel is left open for the potential of unending narrative.

al-Shaykh's *Nights* creates liberating spaces in which social structures can be re-imagined. By following the Shahrazadean technique of repetitious narrative, the novel enables various characters to undermine and re-formulate the very structures of power that restrict them within so-called inferior social and

---

427 Shafak, *Honour*, p. 1.

gender roles. Postcolonial feminine writing is not only demonstrated through
the figure of Shahrazad the storyteller, but it also operates through different
figures and structural mechanisms throughout al-Shaykh's text. Even before
Shahrazad's introduction into the tales as a character, the novel deliberately tries
to disturb the foundation of these patriarchal power structures. The essence of
this undermining lies in how sexual desires are performed and with whom. The
uneasy sexual intimacy between two queens and their slaves calls the patriarchal authority into question. Within the actual scene of adultery, the social and
gender hierarchies are doomed to fail as they are already 'porous [and] fragile'.[428]
By (un)veiling, these slaves can easily transgress both gender and societal norms
as this form of (un)veiling allows them to have sexual intercourse with the king's
wife and concubines. It is the fact that they perform these sexual acts in the
king's garden that makes this act powerful because it indicates the possibility of
getting within patriarchal structures in order to undermine them. It opens up the
potential for both women and the slaves to re-define their social and sexual identities. I therefore suggested that postcolonial feminine writing expands beyond
the figure of Shahrazad within al-Shaykh's *Nights*.

Furthermore, postcolonial feminine writing extends the figure of Shahrazad
through al-Shaykh's presentation of diversely gendered and hybrid bodies.
I argued that postcolonial feminine writing is that which enables al-Shaykh to
rewrite liberating spaces for non-conforming bodies. The novel opens new and
imaginative ways to re-create bodies that do not conform to societal and gendered norms. For instance, the text's portrayal of Zumurrud demonstrates that
the so-called rigid gender and social class structures are indeed fragile and can be
transgressed. Zumurrud's disguise, which is performed as an act of (un)veiling,
challenges these structures by appearing to follow them. Zumurrud's disguise
repeats the act of (un)veiling exhibited by the slaves in the very first scene of
the novel. However, it is different and transgressive precisely because Zumurrud
re-creates a narrative by (un)veiling her body as does Shahrazad. Moreover, the
Nights suggests that bodies cannot be reduced to a single gender and/or social
identity as they are already multiple/hybrid and non-conforming. al-Shaykh
elaborates upon the multiplicity of bodies by re-naming each woman's genitalia
and demonstrates how women can re-define their bodies and that this provides
the potential for agency. In doing so, the text also suggests the possibility for men
to undermine these patriarchal structures if they follow this postcolonial feminine (re)imagining as does the porter in the text.

---

428 Mernissi, *Scheherazade*, p. 46.

While the focus is on bodies and narrative in Chapter I, Chapter II looked at the relationship between the gaze and the narrative through the re-writing of non-conforming bodies in Shafak's *The Gaze*. The text conveys what I am calling postcolonial feminine writing by mirroring the form and narrative techniques of Shahrazad. Shafak perpetually writes and re-writes the same stories in transnational and transhistorical contexts. By repeating these stories, the text posits the potential of re-imagining multiple positions of the gaze. This re-formulation of the gaze unsettles patriarchal and colonial positions of the gaze and offers liberating spaces for marginalised and non-conforming characters the potential to be the subjects of the gaze. These potentialities are what I describe as postcolonial feminine writing.

Postcolonial feminine writing describes how the text creates multiple positions of narrative and the gaze and offers the potential of re-imagining alternative forms of embodiment through the figure of Shahrazad. Similar to al-Shaykh's repetition of the same tales, *The Gaze* repeats the content as well as the characters in order to suggest differing possible endings to these narratives. By the very act of this repetition, the text interrogates the heteronormative embodiment of the characters and allows them to re-create themselves with altered results. By connecting the non-normative characters, B-C and Keramet, and the narrator, the Sable-Girl and Annabelle, *The Gaze* both destabilises narrative boundaries and provides these characters the liberating space to re-define their embodiment and develop their own voices.

The Gaze also expands on the figure of Shahrazad through the act of (un) veiling, which allows the characters to shift between the realms of reality and fantasy as they do gender and social roles. The text portrays how creative use of disguise, as I explored with the form of (un)veiling, can offer a liberating space for characters to act out consensual roles and employ positions of power, even temporarily. By cross-dressing and performing gender non-conforming disguise, both B-C and the fat woman rework their gender identities and divert the gaze that is directed on them. Even if it is a temporary undermining of power dynamics through a reversal of the male gaze, it is this temporary intervention that is repeated in the text and that opens up the potential to find 'hidden crossovers' for transformation of patriarchal power structures.[429]

While Chapter II looked at the potential of voice and the gaze through non-conforming bodies, Chapter III specifically analysed how the restrictive forms of silence and shame can be re-imagined through the lenses of postcolonial feminine

---

429 Cixous, 'Medusa', p. 887.

writing. I looked at how shame is a practice that is reflected on the body and thus becomes an individual and social boundary marker. By re-contextualising shame, I demonstrated that it is not simply a binary opposite to honour, but that it can indeed be re-interpreted as complementing honour, which women may use as a tool of agency. By exploiting the very position of shame, which is reserved for women (and honour for men), this chapter suggested that women can re-write the social norms that rendered their voices 'unthinkable'. In particular, I looked at how shame was proposed as a limiting position for women by patriarchal literary discourses. However, I argued that the novel specifically concentrates on the shame of a woman's body (Jamila) to re-imagine liberating spaces and the potential for her agency. Shame was not a stable social norm as Jamila manipulated it for her own means and used her shame to become a professional midwife. Consequently, this allowed her to hold a position of honour in her society and to transgress boundaries of shame and honour simultaneously.

As a Shahrazadean technique, Chapter III explored silence as a significant part of speech rather than a lack of voice. I argued that *Honour* embraces voice and silence together to recognise the significance of women's silences as much as their voices in contrast to patriarchal interpretations of silence. The fact that this form of expression failed to be recognised by patriarchal authorities did not mean it was any less resistant or powerful. In the event that it was impossible to develop a voice that was not simply submissive to patriarchal authorities, I suggested silences needed 'an intimate listening' to re-formulate new and imaginative ways to exist in society.[430] Then, I argued that the novel portrayed how bodies and other senses such as sight and smell were communicating. Moreover, similar to Shahrazad, who embraced silence at dawn and deferred her narrative until night, *Honour*'s so-called silent characters such as Pembe and Jamila find their voices through Esma's narrative. This does not negate the subversive position of their silences. Rather, I wanted to argue that these silences facilitate and enact another woman's voice by 'the language of 1000 tongues which knows neither enclosure nor death'.[431]

Postcolonial feminine writing offers the potential to get inside of patriarchal literary discourses and intervene in their power structures. This concept provides the ability to re-imagine liberating spaces through which non-conforming bodies can be recognised and re-created. I recognise that these liberating spaces, which are produced through the technique of postcolonial feminine writing that

---

430 McCormack, *Queer Postcolonial Narratives*, p. 181.
431 Cixous, 'Medusa', p. 889.

I have coined (and/or by postcolonial women writers, Shafak and al-Shaykh) are temporary interventions. However, the very repetition of these temporary interventions undermines the stability and restrictiveness of patriarchal power systems and invents more subversive and liberating literary discourses and embodied potentialities.

Bibliography

Aghacy, Samira, 'Lebanese Women's Fiction: Urban Identity and the Tyranny of the Past', *International Journal of Middle East Studies*, 33, 4 (2001), pp. 503–23

Aghacy, Samira, 'Contemporary Lebanese Fiction: Modernization without Modernity', *International Journal of Middle East Studies*, 38, 4 (2006), pp. 561–80

Ahmad, Aijaz, 'The Politics of Literary Postcoloniality', *Race & Class*, 36, 3 (1995), pp. 1–20

Ahmed, Sara, *Strange Encounters: Embodies Others in Post-coloniality* (London: Routledge, 2000)

Ahmed, Sara, *The Cultural Politics of Emotion* (Edinburgh: Edinburgh UP, 2004)

Ahmed, Sara, *Wilful Subjects* (London and Durham, NC: Duke UP, 2014)

Ahmed, Sara, *Living a Feminist Life* (London and Durham, NC: Duke UP, 2017)

Akpinar, Aylin, 'The Honour/Shame Complex Revisited: Violence against Women in the Migration Context', *Women's Studies International Forum*, 26, 5 (2003), pp.425–42

Alaimo, Stacy, *Undomesticated Ground: Recasting Nature as Feminist Space* (Ithaca, NY: Cornell UP, 2000)

Alaimo, Stacy, 'Trans-corporeal Feminisms and the Ethical Space of Nature', in *Material Feminisms*, ed. by Stacy Alaimo and Susan. Hekman (Bloomington, IN: Indiana UP, 2008)

Alaimo, Stacy, and Susan Hekman, *Material Feminisms* (Bloomington, IN: Indiana UP, 2008)

Alaimo, Stacy, *Bodily Natures: Science, Environment and the Material Self* (Bloomington, IN: Indiana UP, 2010)

Alaimo, Stacy, *Exposed: Environmental Politics and Pleasures in Posthuman Times* (Minneapolis, MN: University of Minnesota Press, 2016)

al-Musawi, Muhsin Jassim, *The Postcolonial Arabic Novel: Debating Ambivalence* (Leiden: Brill, 2003)

al-Samman, Hanadi, *Anxiety of Erasure: Trauma, Authorship and the Diaspora in Arab Women's Writings* (Syracuse, NY: Syracuse UP, 2015)

al-Shaykh, Hanan, *One Thousand and One Nights: A New Re-imagining* (London: Bloomsbury, 2011, repr. 2013)

Amireh, Amal, and Lisa Suhair Majaj, *Going Global: The Transnational Reception of the Third World Women Writers* (New York and London: Garland Publishing, 2000)

Aoyagi, Etsuko, 'Repetitiveness in *the Arabian Nights*: Openness as Self-Foundation', in *The Arabian Nights and Orientalism: Perspectives from East and West*, ed. by Yuriko Yamanaka and Tetsuo Nishio (London and New York: I.B. Tauris, 2006), pp. 68–90

Ashcroft, Bill, Gareth Griffiths, and Helen Tiffin, *The Empire Writes Back: Theory and Practice in Postcolonial Literatures* (London and New York: Routledge, 1989, repr. 2002, 2004)

Atayurt-Fenge, Zeynep Z., '"This is a World of Spectacles": Cyclical Narratives and Circular Visionary Formations in Elif Shafak's *The Gaze*', *Critique: Studies in Contemporary Fiction*, 58, 3 (2017), pp. 287–99

Bahrawi, Nazry, 'A Thousand and One Rewrites: Translating Modernity in the Arabian Nights', *Journal of World Literature*, 1, 3 (2016), pp. 357–70

Ball, Anna, 'Things That Walk with Me: Hanan Al-Shaykh in Conversation', *Wasafiri*, 26, 1 (2011), pp. 62–66

Baron, Beth, 'Women, Honour, and the State: Evidence from Egypt', *Middle Eastern Studies*, 42, 1 (2006), pp. 1–20

Bartlett, Alison, 'Thinking through Breasts: Writing Maternity', *Feminist Theory*, 1, 2 (2000), pp. 173–88

Bewes, Timothy, *The Event of Postcolonial Studies* (Princeton, NJ: Princeton UP, 2011)

Bilgiç, Ali, *Turkey, Power and the West: Gendered International Relations and Foreign Policy* (London and New York: I.B. Tauris, 2016)

Bohn, Lauren, '"We're All Handcuffed in This Country." Why Afghanistan Is Still the Worst Place in the World to Be a Woman', *TIME*, 8 December 2018, <https://time.com/5472411/afghanistan-women-justice-war/> [accessed 20 August 2019]

Borges, Jorge Louis, 'The Translators of the *Thousand and One Nights*', in *The Translation Studies Reader*, ed. by Lawrence Venuti (London and New York: Routledge, 2000), pp. 34–48

Bozaslan, Hamit, 'Turkey: Postcolonial Discourse in a Non-colonised State', in *A Historical Companion to Postcolonial Literatures: Continental Europe and Its Empires*, ed. by Prem Poddar et al. (Edinburgh: Edinburgh UP, 2008)

Brandon, James, and Salam Hafez, *Crimes of the Community: Honour-based Violence in the UK* (London: Centre for Social Cohesion CIVITAS, 2008)

Bray, Abigail, *Hélène Cixous: Writing and Sexual Difference* (Basingstoke: Palgrave Macmillan, 2004)

Butler, Judith, *Bodies That Matter* (London and New York: Routledge, 1993, repr. 2011)

Chambers, Claire, *Rivers of Ink: Selected Essays* (Karachi: Oxford UP, 2017)

Chambers, Claire, *Making Sense of Contemporary British Muslim Novels* (London: Palgrave Macmillan, 2019)

Chancy, Myriam J.A., 'Migrations: A Meridians Interview with Elif Shafak', *Meridians: Feminism, Race, Transnationalism*, 4, 1 (2003), pp. 55–85

Cixous, Hélène, *Coming to Writing and Other Essays*, ed. by Deborah Jenson, trans. by Sarah Cornell, Deborah Jenson, Ann Liddle, and Susan Sellers (Cambridge, MA: Harvard UP, 1991)

Cixous, Hélène, 'Sorties: Out and Out: Attacks/Ways Out/Forays', in *The Newly Born Woman*, ed. by Hélène Cixous, and Catherine Clément, trans. by Betsy Wing (London: I.B. Tauris Publishers, 1996), pp. 63–132

Cixous, Hélène, 'The Laugh of Medusa', trans. by Keith Cohen and Paula Cohen, *Signs*, 1, 4 (1976), pp. 875–93

Cixous, Hélène, and Susan Sellers, *White Ink: Interviews on Sex, Text and Politics* (Stocksfield: Acumen, 2008)

Concannon, Kevin, 'Yoko Ono's "Cut Piece": From Text to Performance and Back Again', *PAJ: A Journal of Performance and Art*, 30, 3 (2008), pp. 81–93

Cooke, Miriam, 'Arab Women, Arab Wars', *Cultural Critique*, 29 (1994–95), pp. 5–29

Cooke, Miriam, *Women Claim Islam: Creating Islamic Feminism through Literature* (London and New York: Routledge, 2001)

Davary, Bahar, 'Miss Elsa and the Veil: Honor, Shame, and Identity Negotiations', *Journal of Feminist Studies in Religion*, 25, 2 (2009), pp. 47–66, p. 48

Demirci, Neşe, 'Symbolism of Names in Elif Shafak's *Pinhan, Araf* and *Mahrem*', *Turkish Studies*, 5, 3 (2010), pp. 996–1008

El Hamamsy, Walid, 'Epistolary Memory: Revisiting Traumas in Women's Writing', *Alif: Journal of Comparative Poetics*, 30 (2010), pp. 150–75

El Saadawi, Nawal, *The Hidden Face of Eve* (London: Zed Books, 1980, repr. 2007, 2015)

Fanon, Frantz, *The Wretched of the Earth*, trans. by Constance Farrington (London: Penguin, 2001)

Fanon, Frantz, 'Algeria Unveiled', in *A Dying Colonialism*, trans. by Haakon Chevalier (New York: Grove Press, 1959, 1965), pp. 35–68

Fuery, Patrick, and Nick Mansfield, *Cultural Studies and the New Humanities: Concepts and Controversies* (Melbourne: Oxford UP, 1997)

Furlanetto, Elena, ' "Safe Spaces of the Like-Minded": The Search for a Hybrid Post-Ottoman Identity in Elif Shafak's *The Bastard of Istanbul*', *Commonwealth Essays and Studies*, 36, 2 (2014), pp. 19–31

Fuss, Diana, 'Interior Colonies: Frantz Fanon and the Politics of Identification', in *Rethinking Fanon*, ed. by Nigel Gibson (New York: Humanity Books, 1999), pp. 294–328

Garland-Thomson, Rosemarie, *Freakery: Cultural Spectacles of the Extraordinary Body* (New York and London: New York UP, 1996)

Garland-Thomson, Rosemarie, *Staring: How We Look* (Oxford: Oxford UP, 2009)

Gauch, Suzanne, *Liberating Shahrazad: Feminism, Postcolonialism and Islam* (Minneapolis, MN: The University of Minnesota Press, 2007)

Gilbert, Paul, 'Body Shame: A Biopsychosocial Conceptualisation and Overview with Treatment Implications', in *Body Shame: Conceptualisation, Research and Treatment*, ed. by Paul Gilbert and Jeremy Miles (Hove and New York: Brunner-Routledge, 2002), pp. 3–54

Glenn, Cheryl, *Unspoken: A Rhetoric of Silence* (Carbondale, IL: Southern Illinois UP, 2004)

Golban, Tatiana 'The Migrant Hero's Boundaries of Masculine Honour Code in Elif Shafak's *Honour*', in *Culture, Literature and Migration*, ed. by Ali Tilbe, and Rania M. Rafik Khalil (London: Transnational Press, 2019), pp. 103–18

Göçek, Fatma Müge, *Political Cartoons in the Middle East* (Princeton, NJ: Markus Wiener Publishers, 1998)

Haddawy, Husain, 'Introduction', in *The Arabian Nights*, ed. by Muhsin Mahdi (New York and London: W.W. Norton & Company, 1990)

Haugbolle, Sune, *War and Memory in Lebanon* (Cambridge: Cambridge UP, 2010)

Hegde, Radha S., 'Narratives of Silence: Rethinking Gender, Agency, and Power from the Communication Experiences of Battered Women in South India', *Communication Studies*, 47, 4 (1996), pp. 303–17

Helie Lucas, Marie-Aimee, 'Women, Nationalism and Religion in the Algerian Liberation Struggle', in *Rethinking Fanon*, ed. by Nigel Gibson (New York: Humanity Books, 1999), pp. 271–82

Hird, Myra J., 'Naturally Queer', *Feminist Theory*, 5, 1 (2004), pp. 85–89

Hout, Syrine, *Post-war Anglophone Lebanese Fiction: Home Matters in the Diaspora* (Edinburgh: Edinburgh UP, 2012)

Irigaray, Luce, *This Sex Which Is Not One*, trans. by Catherine Porter (Ithaca, NY: Cornell UP, 1985)

Ivanova, Petya Tsoneva, *Negotiating Borderlines in Four Contemporary Migrant Writers from the Middle East* (Newcastle upon Tyne: Cambridge Scholars Publishing, 2018)

Jones, Ann Rosalind, 'Writing the Body: Toward an Understanding of "L'Ecriture Feminine"', *Feminist Studies*, 7, 2 (1981), pp. 247–63

Jones, Ann Rosalind, 'Inscribing Femininity: French Theories of the Feminine', in *Making A Difference: Feminist Literary Criticism*, ed. by Gayle Green and Coppelia Kahn (London: Routledge, 1985), pp. 80–112

Kandiyoti, Deniz, 'End of Empire: Islam, Nationalism and Women in Turkey', in *Women, Islam and the State*, ed. by Deniz Kandiyoti (Philadelphia, PA: Temple UP, 1991)

Kaplan, E. Ann, *Looking for the Other: Feminism, Film and the Imperial Gaze* (London and New York: Routledge, 1997)

Kaufman, Gershen, *Shame: The Power of Caring* (Cambridge, MA: Schenkman, 1980)

Kellaway, Kate, 'Interview: Elif Shafak', *The Guardian*, 5th Feb 2017, <https://www.theguardian.com/books/2017/feb/05/elif-shafak-turkey-three-daughters-of-eve-interview> [accessed 15th Jan 2019]

Khan, Nuzhat, 'Accountability in Honour Killings: Reading of Elif Shafak's *Honour*', *PARIPEX – Indian Journal of Research*, 6, 6 (2017), pp. 477–80

Kushal, Shweta, and Evangeline Manickam, '(Dis)honourable Paradigms: A Critical Reading of *Provoked*, *Shame* and *Daughters of Shame*', *South Asian Diaspora*, 6, 2 (2014), pp. 225–38

Lacan, Jacques, *Book XI: The Four Fundamental Concepts of Psychoanalysis*, ed. by Jacques-Alain Miller, trans. by Alan Sheridan (New York and London: W.W. Norton & Company, 1981, repr. 1998)

Landry, Donna, 'Queer Islam and New Historicism', *Cultural Studies*, 25, 2 (2011), pp. 147–63

Larson, Charles R., 'The Fiction of Hanan al-Shaykh, Reluctant Feminist', *World Literature Today*, 65, 1 (1991), pp. 14–7

Lee, Robert G., and Gordon Wheeler, *The Voice of Shame: Silence and Connection in Psychotherapy* (Cambridge, MA: GestaltPress, 1996, repr. 2003)

Lewis, Bernard, *The Multiple Identities of the Middle East* (New York: Schocken Books, 1998, 1999)

Majaj, Lisa Suahir, Paula W. Sunderman, and Therese Saliba, *Intersections: Gender, Nation, and Community in Arab Women's Novels* (Syracuse, NY: Syracuse UP, 2002)

Malti-Douglas, Fedwa, *Woman's Body, Woman's Word: Gender and Discourse in Arabo-Islamic Writing* (Princeton, NJ: Princeton UP, 1991)

Marks, Laura U., *Touch: Sensuous Theory and Multisensory Media* (Minneapolis, MN: The University of Minnesota Press, 2002)

Marroum, Marianne, 'What's So Great About Home?: Roots, Nostalgia, and Return in Andree Chedid's *La Maison sans racines* and Hanan al-Shaykh's *Hikayat Zahra*', *Comparative Literature Studies*, 45, 4 (2008), pp. 491–513

Matthes, Melissa, 'Shahrazad's Sisters: Storytelling and Politics in the Memoirs of Mernissi, el Saadawi and Ashrawi', *Alif: Journal of Comparative Poetics*, 19 (1999), pp. 68–96

McArdle, Molly, 'Author Q&A: Hanan al-Shaykh's New Shahrazad', *L J Reviews*, 26th April 2013, < http://www.libraryjournal.com/?detailStory=author-qa-hanan-al-shaykhs-new-shahrazad > [accessed 2nd October 2021]

McClintock, Anne, *Imperial Leather: Race, Gender and Sexuality in the Colonial Contest* (New York: Routledge, 1995)

McCormack, Donna, 'Gender and Colonial Transitioning: Frantz Fanon's Algerian Freedom Fighters in Moroccan and Caribbean Novels?', *Journal of Transatlantic Studies*, 7, 3 (2009), pp. 279–93

McCormack, Donna, *Queer Postcolonial Narratives and the Ethics of Witnessing* (London and New York: Bloomsbury, 2015)

McLeod, John, *Beginning Postcolonialism* (Manchester: Manchester UP, 2000)

Mernissi, Fatema, *Scheherazade Goes West: Different Cultures, Different Harems* (Washington Square Press: New York, 2001)

Mitra, Namrata, 'Shamed Bodies: Partition Violence and Women', in *The Female Face of Shame*, ed. by Erica L. Johnson, and Patricia Moran (Bloomington, IN: Indiana UP, 2013)

Moore, Lindsey, ' "Darkly as through a Veil": Reading Representations of Algerian Women', *Intercultural Education*, 18, 4 (2007), pp. 335–51

Moore, Lindsey, *Arab, Muslim, Woman: Voice and Vision in Postcolonial Literature and Film* (Abingdon and New York: Routledge, 2008)

Naddaff, Sandra, *Arabesque: Narrative Structure and the Aesthetics of Repetition in 1001 Nights* (Evanston, IL: Northwestern UP, 1991)

Newman, Beth, 'Getting Fixed: Feminine Identity and Scopic Crisis in *The Turn of the Screw*', *Novel*, 26, 1 (1992), pp. 43–63

O'Riley, Michael, 'Specters of Orientalism in France, Algeria, and Postcolonial Studies', *Mosaic*, 34, 4 (2001), pp. 47–64

Ramakrishnan, A.K., 'The Gaze of Orientalism: Reflections on Linking Postcolonialism and International Relations' *International Studies*, 36 (1999), pp. 129–63

Sabry, Somaya Sami, *Arab-American Women's Writing and Performance: Orientalism, Race and the Idea of The Arabian Nights* (I.B. Tauris: New York, 2011)

Sabry, Somaya Sami, 'Performing Sheherazade: Arab-American Women's Contestations of Identity', *Alif: Journal of Comparative Poetics*, 31 (2011), pp. 196–219

Said, Edward W., *Orientalism* (New York: Vintage Books, 1978, repr. 1979)

Salem, Elise, 'Patricia Sarrafian Ward, *The Bullet Collection*', *Literary Review*, 46, 4 (2003), pp. 769–70

Scarry, Elaine, *The Body in Pain: The Making and Unmaking of the World* (Oxford: Oxford UP, 1985)

Schutte, Gillian, 'The Laugh of Medusa Heard in South African Women's Poetry', *Scrunity2*, 16, 2 (2011), pp. 42–55

Sellers, Susan, *Language and Sexual Difference: Feminist Writing in France* (New York: Macmillan Education, 1991)

Sellers, Susan, 'On Hélène Cixous's "The Laugh of Medusa"', *Women: A Cultural Review*, 21, 1 (2010), pp. 22–5Shafak, Elif, *Honour* (London: Penguin, 2013)

Shafak, Elif, *The Gaze*, trans. by Brendan Freely (London: Penguin, 2010)

Shafak, Elif, *Black Milk: On the Conflicting Demands of Writing, Creativity, and Motherhood*, trans. by Hande Zapsu (London: Penguin, 2007)

Shafak, Elif, 'Storytelling, Fake Worlds, and the Internet', *World Literature Today*, 89, 1 (2015), pp. 39–41

Shafak, Elif, 'The Politics of Fiction', online video recording, *TedTalk*, July 2010, <https://www.ted.com/talks/elif_shafak_the_politics_of_fiction> [accessed 28th December 2019]

Shafak, Elif, 'The Revolutionary Power of Diverse Thought', online video recording, *TEDTalk*, September 2017, <https://www.ted.com/talks/elif_shafak_the_revolutionary_power_of_diverse_thought?language=en> [accessed 28th December 2019]

Shafak, Elif, 'As a Lost Child in Turkey I Found Refuge on an Imaginary Mountain', *The Guardian*, 26th August 2019, <https://www.theguardian.com/commentisfree/2019/aug/26/lost-child-turkey-refuge-imaginary-mountain> [accessed 5th December 2019]

Sunderman, Paula, 'An Interview with Hanan al-Shaykh', *Michigan Quarterly Review*, 31, 4 (1992), pp. 625–36

Tagore, Proma, *The Shapes of Silence* (Montreal and Kingston: McGill-Queen's UP, 2009)

Valassopoulos, Anastasia, *Contemporary Arab Women Writers: Cultural Expression in Context* (London and New York: Routledge, 2007)

Viner, Katherine, 'Feminism as Imperialism', *The Guardian*, 21st September 2002, <http://www.theguardian.com/world/2002/sep/21/gender.usa> [accessed 20 August 2019]

Visweswaran, Kamala, *Fictions of Feminist Ethnography* (Minneapolis, MN: The University of Minnesota Press, 1994)

Werbner, Pnina, 'Veiled interventions in Pure Space: Honour, Shame and Embodied Struggles among Muslims in Britain and France', *Theory, Culture and Society*, 24, 2 (2007), pp. 161–86

Yeğenoğlu, Meyda, *Colonial Fantasies: Towards a Feminist Reading of Orientalism* (Cambridge: Cambridge UP, 1998, repr. 2001)

Young, Robert J.C., 'What is the Postcolonial', *ARIEL*, 40, 1 (2009), pp. 13–25

Index

www.ingramcontent.com/pod-product-compliance
Lightning Source LLC
Chambersburg PA
CBHW050611280326
41932CB00016B/2998